| The Holocaust

Titles in the Genocide and Persecution Series

Afghanistan
Argentina
Armenia
Bosnia
Burma
Cambodia
Chile
Darfur
East Pakistan
El Salvador and Guatemala
The Holocaust
Indonesia
Kosovo
The Kurds
Liberia
Namibia
The People's Republic of China
The Romani
Russia
Rwanda
South Africa
Sri Lanka
Tibet
Uganda

# GENOCIDE & PERSECUTION

| The Holocaust

Jeff Hay
Book Editor

Frank Chalk
Consulting Editor

GREENHAVEN PRESS
A part of Gale, Cengage Learning

Farmington Hills, Mich • San Francisco • New York • Waterville, Maine
Meriden, Conn • Mason, Ohio • Chicago

Elizabeth Des Chenes, *Director, Content Strategy*
Cynthia Sanner, *Publisher*
Douglas Dentino, *Manager, New Product*

© 2014 Greenhaven Press, a part of Gale, Cengage Learning

WCN: 01-100-101

Gale and Greenhaven Press are registered trademarks used herein under license.

For more information, contact:
Greenhaven Press
27500 Drake Rd.
Farmington Hills, MI 48331-3535
Or you can visit our Internet site at gale.cengage.com.

ALL RIGHTS RESERVED
No part of this work covered by the copyright herein may be reproduced, transmitted, stored, or used in any form or by any means graphic, electronic, or mechanical, including but not limited to photocopying, recording, scanning, digitizing, taping, Web distribution, information networks, or information storage and retrieval systems, except as permitted under Section 107 or 108 of the 1976 United States Copyright Act, without the prior written permission of the publisher.

For product information and technology assistance, contact us at:

Gale Customer Support, 1-800-877-4253
For permission to use material from this text or product, submit all requests online at www.cengage.com/permissions

Further permissions questions can be emailed to permissionrequest@cengage.com

Every effort is made to ensure that Greenhaven Press accurately reflects the original intent of the authors. Every effort has been made to trace the owners of copyrighted material.

Cover image © posztos/Shutterstock.com.
Interior barbed wire artwork © f9photos, used under license from Shutterstock.com.

LIBRARY OF CONGRESS CATALOGING-IN-PUBLICATION DATA

The Holocaust / Jeff Hay, book editor.
   pages cm -- (Genocide and persecution)
   Summary: "Genocide and Persecution: The Holocaust: Each Genocide and Persecution title focuses on a single instance of genocide, crimes against humanity, or severe persecution"-- Provided by publisher.
   Includes bibliographical references and index.
   ISBN 978-0-7377-6897-8 (hardback)
1. Holocaust, Jewish (1939-1945)--Juvenile literature. I. Hay, Jeff, editor of compilation.
   D804.34.H644 2013
   940.53'18--dc23
                                                                      2013046379

Printed in the United States of America
1 2 3 4 5 6 7 18 17 16 15 14

Contents

Preface	1
Foreword	5
World Map	15
Chronology	18

Chapter 1: The History of the Holocaust

Chapter Exercises   26

1. An Overview of the Holocaust   28
   Christian Gerlach

   A scholar examines the origins of the Holocaust, the means by which Nazi Germany carried it out, and some of the debates it has inspired.

2. A 1938 Pogrom Against German Jews Was an Important Step Toward the Holocaust   41
   Anonymous

   In November 1938 Nazi officials staged a nationwide attack on German homes, businesses, and synagogues. An unidentified writer from the American Holocaust Museum describes the event, which is often referred to as Kristallnacht, or the Night of Broken Glass.

3. The Holocaust Began with Mass Shootings on the Eastern Front   48
   Doris L. Bergen

   A historian examines how German forces first began killing large numbers of Jews using mobile execution squads who followed Germany's armed forces in their 1941 invasion of Soviet Russia.

4. German Officials Discuss the "Final Solution to the Jewish Question"   58
   Wannsee Protocol and Adolf Eichmann

   The Nazi's decision to try to massacre Europe's Jews, as opposed to encouraging or forcing them to emigrate, became, in effect, the official policy of the state with the Wannsee Conference of January 20, 1942.

5. The Holocaust Just Got More Shocking　　　　　　　67
   Eric Lichtblau

   Although most of the genocide during the Holocaust took place in mass shooting operations or in special extermination camps, Nazi Germany also constructed hundreds of ghettos, slave labor camps, prisons, and other such facilities. A US journalist reports on recent research into the extent of Nazi efforts.

6. Modern Students Visit One of the Death Camps of the Holocaust　　　　　　　72
   Will Oliphant

   A British journalist reports on a journey by two hundred high school students to the Auschwitz extermination camp in Poland, a trip taken so that these students could be exposed to the horrors of the Holocaust firsthand.

7. Special Efforts Have Been Made in Both Israel and the United States to Keep the Memory of the Holocaust Alive　　　　　　　76
   Norman J.W. Goda

   Governmental organizations, museums, and other institutions continue to inform and educate on the magnitude and horror of the Holocaust.

Chapter 2: Controversies and Perspectives
Chapter Exercises　　　　　　　84
1. Adolf Hitler Always Planned to Rid Europe of Jews　　86
   Kevin P. Sweeney

   A scholar argues that it was always Hitler's intention to eliminate Jews from Europe.

2. The Holocaust Began Because of Circumstances Rather than a Longstanding Plan　　　　　　　95
   Gordon McFee

   Noting the importance of Adolf Hitler himself approving of the measures, a historian suggests that, rather than fulfilling a longstanding plan, the Nazis only decided to try to massacre Europe's Jews in late 1941.

3. Only the Pressures of War Turned Ordinary
   Germans into Killers   101
   Christopher R. Browning

   Instead of being enthusiastic killers, a scholar writes, Nazi police only adjusted themselves to murderous duties because of orders, peer pressure, and other circumstances of war.

4. It Is Important to Keep Alive the Memory of the
   Holocaust in the Face of Challenges   108
   Sean Lang

   A historian argues that it remains important to learn the lessons of the Holocaust, despite the passage of time and the fact that its events are questioned in some circles.

5. Holocaust Deniers Often Try to Appear Respectable   113
   Nick Ryan

   Although their claims are both easy to refute and an insult to victims, a British journalist argues, that those who deny the truth of the Holocaust use the illusion of "academic respectability" to try to keep a false controversy alive.

6. A Holocaust Denier Loses in Court   119
   Douglas Davis

   In 2000 a prominent British historian who had taken to denying that the Holocaust occurred lost a libel case against an American Holocaust scholar. The verdict served as testimony to the continued challenge of Holocaust denial.

Chapter 3: Personal Narratives

Chapter Exercises   126

1. A Survivor Recounts His Capture and His Journey
   to the Auschwitz Extermination Camp   127
   Primo Levi

An Italian Jew, turned over to German forces in late 1943, describes his reactions and those of other victims as they are gathered together and exiled to a Nazi death camp, a place about which they knew nothing.

2. Watching the Departure of Ghetto Children to One of Nazi Germany's Death Camps 136
   Oscar Singer

   Among the first to be sent to extermination camps were Polish Jews who had already been crammed into overcrowded, unsanitary ghettos. A writer recounts the scene when, in the orderly fashion of Nazi Germany, children were sent away from the ghetto located in the city of Lodz.

3. The Horrors of the Holocaust Included Medical Experiments on Young Prisoners 140
   Zoe Johannsen

   In a brief interview conducted by an American eighth grader, a Holocaust survivor remembers losing her parents and being used, along with her twin sister, in medical experiments at Auschwitz.

4. Surviving the Warsaw Ghetto, Auschwitz, and the Death Marches 145
   Solomon Radasky

   A Warsaw shopkeeper remembers that city's ghetto and gas chambers, and the slave labor centers of Auschwitz.

5. An American Jewish Woman, Originally from Hungary, Recalls Her Experiences 155
   Leo Adam Biga

   Only nineteen when her terrors began, a Jewish woman who was deported by the Nazis to Auschwitz, the largest of the death camps, remembers how the experience changed her life.

6. A Soldier Remembers the Liberation of One of Hitler's Camps 166
   Phil Davison

Only the end of World War II revealed to the outside world the true extent and nature of the Holocaust. A British soldier tells of his unit's entry into Bergen-Belsen, a German concentration camp where many Holocaust survivors were abandoned.

Glossary	169
Organizations to Contact	172
List of Primary Source Documents	176
For Further Research	179
Index	183

Preface

> *"For the dead and the living, we must bear witness."*
>
> Elie Wiesel, Nobel laureate and Holocaust survivor

The histories of many nations are shaped by horrific events involving torture, violent repression, and systematic mass killings. The inhumanity of such events is difficult to comprehend, yet understanding why such events take place, what impact they have on society, and how they may be prevented in the future is vitally important. The Genocide and Persecution series provides readers with anthologies of previously published materials on acts of genocide, crimes against humanity, and other instances of extreme persecution, with an emphasis on events taking place in the twentieth and twenty-first centuries. The series offers essential historical background on these significant events in modern world history, presents the issues and controversies surrounding the events, and provides first-person narratives from people whose lives were altered by the events. By providing primary sources, as well as analysis of crucial issues, these volumes help develop critical-thinking skills and support global connections. In addition, the series directly addresses curriculum standards focused on informational text and literary nonfiction and explicitly promotes literacy in history and social studies.

Each Genocide and Persecution volume focuses on genocide, crimes against humanity, or severe persecution. Material from a variety of primary and secondary sources presents a multinational perspective on the event. Articles are carefully edited and introduced to provide context for readers. The series includes volumes on significant and widely studied events like the Holocaust, as well as events that are less often studied, such as the East Pakistan genocide in what is now Bangladesh. Some volumes focus on multiple events endured by a specific people, such as the Kurds, or multiple events enacted over time by a particular oppressor or in a particular location, such as the People's Republic of China.

Each volume is organized into three chapters. The first chapter provides readers with general background information and uses primary sources such as testimony from tribunals or international courts, documents or speeches from world leaders, and legislative text. The second chapter presents multinational perspectives on issues and controversies and addresses current implications or long-lasting effects of the event. Viewpoints explore such topics as root causes; outside interventions, if any; the impact on the targeted group and the region; and the contentious issues that arose in the aftermath. The third chapter presents first-person narratives from affected people, including survivors, family members of victims, perpetrators, officials, aid workers, and other witnesses.

In addition, numerous features are included in each volume of Genocide and Persecution:

- An annotated **table of contents** provides a brief summary of each essay in the volume.
- A **foreword** gives important background information on the recognition, definition, and study of genocide in recent history and examines current efforts focused on the prevention of future atrocities.
- A **chronology** offers important dates leading up to, during, and following the event.
- **Primary sources**—including historical newspaper accounts, testimony, and personal narratives—are among the varied selections in the anthology.
- **Illustrations**—including a world map, photographs, charts, graphs, statistics, and tables—are closely tied

to the text and chosen to help readers understand key points or concepts.
- **Sidebars**—including biographies of key figures and overviews of earlier or related historical events—offer additional content.
- **Pedagogical features**—including analytical exercises, writing prompts, and group activities—introduce each chapter and help reinforce the material. These features promote proficiency in writing, speaking, and listening skills and literacy in history and social studies.
- A **glossary** defines key terms, as needed.
- An annotated list of international **organizations to contact** presents sources of additional information on the volume topic.
- A **list of primary source documents** provides an annotated list of reports, treaties, resolutions, and judicial decisions related to the volume topic.
- A **for further research** section offers a bibliography of books, periodical articles, and Internet sources and an annotated section of other items such as films and websites.
- A comprehensive subject **index** provides access to key people, places, events, and subjects cited in the text.

The Genocide and Persecution series illuminates atrocities that cannot and should not be forgotten. By delving deeply into these events from a variety of perspectives, students and other readers are provided with the information they need to think critically about the past and its implications for the future.

Foreword

The term *genocide* often appears in news stories and other literature. It is not widely known, however, that the core meaning of the term comes from a legal definition, and the concept became part of international criminal law only in 1951 when the United Nations Convention on the Prevention and Punishment of the Crime of Genocide came into force. The word *genocide* appeared in print for the first time in 1944 when Raphael Lemkin, a Polish Jewish refugee from Adolf Hitler's World War II invasion of Eastern Europe, invented the term and explored its meaning in his pioneering book *Axis Rule in Occupied Europe*.

Humanity's Recognition of Genocide and Persecution

Lemkin understood that throughout the history of the human race there have always been leaders who thought they could solve their problems not only through victory in war, but also by destroying entire national, ethnic, racial, or religious groups. Such annihilations of entire groups, in Lemkin's view, deprive the world of the very cultural diversity and richness in languages, traditions, values, and practices that distinguish the human race from all other life on earth. Genocide is not only unjust, it threatens the very existence and progress of human civilization, in Lemkin's eyes.

Looking to the past, Lemkin understood that the prevailing coarseness and brutality of earlier human societies and the lower value placed on human life obscured the existence of genocide. Sacrifice and exploitation, as well as torture and public execution, had been common at different times in history. Looking toward a more humane future, Lemkin asserted the need to punish—and when possible prevent—a crime for which there had been no name until he invented it.

Legal Definitions of Genocide

On December 9, 1948, the United Nations adopted its Convention on the Prevention and Punishment of the Crime of Genocide (UNGC). Under Article II, genocide

> means any of the following acts committed with intent to destroy, in whole or in part, a national, ethnical, racial or religious group, as such:
> (a) Killing members of the group;
> (b) Causing serious bodily or mental harm to members of the group;
> (c) Deliberately inflicting on the group conditions of life calculated to bring about its physical destruction in whole or in part;
> (d) Imposing measures intended to prevent births within the group;
> (e) Forcibly transferring children of the group to another group.

Article III of the convention defines the elements of the crime of genocide, making punishable:

> (a) Genocide;
> (b) Conspiracy to commit genocide;
> (c) Direct and public incitement to commit genocide;
> (d) Attempt to commit genocide;
> (e) Complicity in genocide.

After intense debate, the architects of the convention excluded acts committed with intent to destroy social, political, and economic groups from the definition of genocide. Thus, attempts to destroy whole social classes—the physically and mentally challenged, and homosexuals, for example—are not acts of genocide under the terms of the UNGC. These groups achieved a belated but very significant measure of protection under international criminal law in the Rome Statute of the International Criminal

Foreword

Court, adopted at a conference on July 17, 1998, and entered into force on July 1, 2002.

The Rome Statute defined a crime against humanity in the following way:

> any of the following acts when committed as part of a widespread and systematic attack directed against any civilian population:
>
> (a) Murder;
>
> (b) Extermination;
>
> (c) Enslavement;
>
> (d) Deportation or forcible transfer of population;
>
> (e) Imprisonment or other severe deprivation of physical liberty in violation of fundamental rules of international law;
>
> (f) Torture;
>
> (g) Rape, sexual slavery, enforced prostitution, forced pregnancy, enforced sterilization, or any other form of sexual violence of comparable gravity;
>
> (h) Persecution against any identifiable group or collectivity on political, racial, national, ethnic, cultural, religious, gender . . . or other grounds that are universally recognized as impermissible under international law, in connection with any act referred to in this paragraph or any crime within the jurisdiction of this Court;
>
> (i) Enforced disappearance of persons;
>
> (j) The crime of apartheid;
>
> (k) Other inhumane acts of a similar character intentionally causing great suffering, or serious injury to body or to mental or physical health.

Although genocide is often ranked as "the crime of crimes," in practice prosecutors find it much easier to convict perpetrators of crimes against humanity rather than genocide under domestic laws. However, while Article I of the UNGC declares that countries adhering to the UNGC recognize genocide as "a crime under international law which they undertake to prevent and to punish," the Rome Statute provides no comparable international mechanism for the prosecution of crimes against humanity. A treaty would help individual countries and international institutions introduce measures to prevent crimes against humanity, as well as open more avenues to the domestic and international prosecution of war criminals.

The Evolving Laws of Genocide

In the aftermath of the serious crimes committed against civilians in the former Yugoslavia since 1991 and the Rwanda genocide of 1994, the United Nations Security Council created special international courts to bring the alleged perpetrators of these events to justice. While the UNGC stands as the standard definition of genocide in law, the new courts contributed significantly to today's nuanced meaning of genocide, crimes against humanity, ethnic cleansing, and serious war crimes in international criminal law.

Also helping to shape contemporary interpretations of such mass atrocity crimes are the special and mixed courts for Sierra Leone, Cambodia, Lebanon, and Iraq, which may be the last of their type in light of the creation of the International Criminal Court (ICC), with its broad jurisdiction over mass atrocity crimes in all countries that adhere to the Rome Statute of the ICC. The Yugoslavia and Rwanda tribunals have already clarified the law of genocide, ruling that rape can be prosecuted as a weapon in committing genocide, evidence of intent can be absent when convicting low-level perpetrators of genocide, and public incitement to commit genocide is a crime even if genocide does not immediately follow the incitement.

Several current controversies about genocide are worth noting and will require more research in the future:

1. Dictators accused of committing genocide or persecution may hold onto power more tightly for fear of becoming

vulnerable to prosecution after they step down. Therefore, do threats of international indictments of these alleged perpetrators actually delay transfers of power to more representative rulers, thereby causing needless suffering?
2. Would the large sum of money spent for international retributive justice be better spent on projects directly benefiting the survivors of genocide and persecution?
3. Can international courts render justice impartially or do they deliver only "victors' justice," that is the application of one set of rules to judge the vanquished and a different and laxer set of rules to judge the victors?

It is important to recognize that the law of genocide is constantly evolving, and scholars searching for the roots and early warning signs of genocide may prefer to use their own definitions of genocide in their work. While the UNGC stands as the standard definition of genocide in law, the debate over its interpretation and application will never end. The ultimate measure of the value of any definition of genocide is its utility for identifying the roots of genocide and preventing future genocides.

Motives for Genocide and Early Warning Signs

When identifying past cases of genocide, many scholars work with some version of the typology of motives published in 1990 by historian Frank Chalk and sociologist Kurt Jonassohn in their book *The History and Sociology of Genocide*. The authors identify the following four motives and acknowledge that they may overlap, or several lesser motives might also drive a perpetrator:

1. To eliminate a real or potential threat, as in Imperial Rome's decision to annihilate Carthage in 146 BC.
2. To spread terror among real or potential enemies, as in Genghis Khan's destruction of city-states and people who rebelled against the Mongols in the thirteenth century.

3. To acquire economic wealth, as in the case of the Massachusetts Puritans' annihilation of the native Pequot people in 1637.
4. To implement a belief, theory, or an ideology, as in the case of Germany's decision under Hitler and the Nazis to destroy completely the Jewish people of Europe from 1941 to 1945.

Although these motives represent differing goals, they share common early warning signs of genocide. A good example of genocide in recent times that could have been prevented through close attention to early warning signs was the genocide of 1994 inflicted on the people labeled as "Tutsi" in Rwanda. Between 1959 and 1963, the predominantly Hutu political parties in power stigmatized all Tutsi as members of a hostile racial group, violently forcing their leaders and many civilians into exile in neighboring countries through a series of assassinations and massacres. Despite systematic exclusion of Tutsi from service in the military, government security agencies, and public service, as well as systematic discrimination against them in higher education, hundreds of thousands of Tutsi did remain behind in Rwanda. Government-issued cards identified each Rwandan as Hutu or Tutsi.

A generation later, some Tutsi raised in refugee camps in Uganda and elsewhere joined together, first organizing politically and then militarily, to reclaim a place in their homeland. When the predominantly Tutsi Rwanda Patriotic Front invaded Rwanda from Uganda in October 1990, extremist Hutu political parties demonized all of Rwanda's Tutsi as traitors, ratcheting up hate propaganda through radio broadcasts on government-run Radio Rwanda and privately owned radio station RTLM. Within the print media, *Kangura* and other publications used vicious cartoons to further demonize Tutsi and to stigmatize any Hutu who dared advocate bringing Tutsi into the government. Massacres of dozens and later hundreds of Tutsi sprang up even as Rwandans prepared to elect a coalition government led by moderate political parties, and as the United Nations dispatched a small international military force led by Canadian general Roméo Dallaire to oversee the elections and political transition. Late in 1992, an international human rights organization's investigating team detected the hate propaganda campaign, verified systematic massacres of Tutsi, and warned the international community that Rwanda had already entered the early stages of genocide, to no avail. On April 6, 1994, Rwanda's genocidal killing accelerated at an alarming pace when someone shot down the airplane flying Rwandan president Juvenal Habyarimana home from peace talks in Arusha, Tanzania.

Hundreds of thousands of Tutsi civilians—including children, women, and the elderly—died horrible deaths because the world ignored the early warning signs of the genocide and refused to act. Prominent among those early warning signs were: 1) systematic, government-decreed discrimination against the Tutsi as members of a supposed racial group; 2) government-issued identity cards labeling every Tutsi as a member of a racial group; 3) hate propaganda casting all Tutsi as subversives and traitors; 4) organized assassinations and massacres targeting Tutsi; and 5) indoctrination of militias and special military units to believe that all Tutsi posed a genocidal threat to the existence of Hutu and would enslave Hutu if they ever again became the rulers of Rwanda.

Genocide Prevention and the Responsibility to Protect

The shock waves emanating from the Rwanda genocide forced world leaders at least to acknowledge in principle that the national sovereignty of offending nations cannot trump the responsibility of those governments to prevent the infliction of mass atrocities on their own people. When governments violate that obligation, the member states of the United Nations have a responsibility to get involved. Such involvement can take the form of, first, offering to help the local government change its ways through technical advice and development aid, and second—if the local government persists in assaulting its own people—initiating armed intervention to protect the civilians at risk. In 2005 the United Nations began to implement the Responsibility to Protect initiative, a framework of principles to guide the international community in preventing mass atrocities.

As in many real-world domains, theory and practice often diverge. Genocide and crimes against humanity are rooted in problems that produce failing states: poverty, poor education, extreme nationalism, lawlessness, dictatorship, and corruption. Implementing the principles of the Responsibility to Protect doctrine burdens intervening state leaders with the necessity of addressing each of those problems over a long period of time. And when those problems prove too intractable and complex to solve easily, the citizens of the intervening nations may lose patience, voting out the leader who initiated the intervention. Arguments based solely on humanitarian principles fail to overcome such concerns. What is needed to persuade political leaders to stop preventable mass atrocities are compelling arguments based on their own national interests.

Preventable mass atrocities threaten the national interests of all states in five specific ways:

1. Mass atrocities create conditions that engender widespread and concrete threats from terrorism, piracy, and other forms of lawlessness on the land and sea;
2. Mass atrocities facilitate the spread of warlordism, whose tentacles block affordable access to vital raw materials produced in the affected country and threaten the prosperity of all nations that depend on the consumption of these resources;
3. Mass atrocities trigger cascades of refugees and internally displaced populations that, combined with climate change and growing international air travel, will accelerate the worldwide incidence of lethal infectious diseases;

4. Mass atrocities spawn single-interest parties and political agendas that drown out more diverse political discourse in the countries where the atrocities take place and in the countries that host large numbers of refugees. Xenophobia and nationalist backlashes are the predictable consequences of government indifference to mass atrocities elsewhere that could have been prevented through early actions;
5. Mass atrocities foster the spread of national and transnational criminal networks trafficking in drugs, women, arms, contraband, and laundered money.

Alerting elected political representatives to the consequences of mass atrocities should be part of every student movement's agenda in the twenty-first century. Adam Smith, the great political economist and author of *The Wealth of Nations*, put it best when he wrote: "It is not from the benevolence of the butcher, the brewer, or the baker that we expect our dinner, but from their regard to their own interest." Self-interest is a powerful engine for good in the marketplace and can be an equally powerful motive and source of inspiration for state action to prevent genocide and mass persecution. In today's new global village, the lives we save may be our own.

Frank Chalk

Frank Chalk, who has a doctorate from the University of Wisconsin-Madison, is a professor of history and director of the Montreal Institute for Genocide and Human Rights Studies at Concordia University in Montreal, Canada. He is coauthor, with Kurt

Jonassohn, of The History and Sociology of Genocide *(1990); coauthor with General Roméo Dallaire, Kyle Matthews, Carla Barqueiro, and Simon Doyle of* Mobilizing the Will to Intervene: Leadership to Prevent Mass Atrocities *(2010); and associate editor of the three-volume Macmillan Reference USA* Encyclopedia of Genocide and Crimes Against Humanity *(2004). Chalk served as president of the International Association of Genocide Scholars from June 1999 to June 2001. His current research focuses on the use of radio and television broadcasting in the incitement and prevention of genocide, and domestic laws on genocide. For more information on genocide and examples of the experiences of people displaced by genocide and other human rights violations, interested readers can consult the websites of the Montreal Institute for Genocide and Human Rights Studies (http://migs.concordia.ca) and the Montreal Life Stories project (www.lifestoriesmontreal.ca).*

World Map

Chronology

September 1919 World War I veteran Adolf Hitler joins a political organization that soon becomes the Nazi Party.

1921 Now leader of the Nazi Party, Hitler announces the party's "25-Point Plan," which includes the assertion that Jews could never be "members of the German nation."

1925 Hitler publishes the manifesto *Mein Kampf* in which he describes the threat he feels Jews represent to his dreams for Europe, as well as his visions of another large European war.

January 1933 Hitler achieves power as chancellor of Germany and, thereafter, takes steps to turn the nation into a one-party dictatorship.

March 1933 Dachau, the first major concentration camp, is opened. Its first prisoners are political opponents to Nazism.

April 1933 The Nazi government tries—and fails—to institute a nationwide boycott on Jewish businesses.

The first of a set of civil service acts removes Jews from government jobs in Germany.

September 1935 The Nuremburg Laws remove citizenship rights from German Jews and ban mar-

	riage or sexual activity between Jews and Aryan Germans.
March 1938	Nazi Germany annexes Austria in the so-called *Anschluss* (connection), placing nearly 150,000 additional Jews under Nazi control.
August 1938	The first Schutzstaffel (SS) Office for Jewish Emigration opens in Vienna, Austria, under Adolf Eichmann, helping Eichmann to gain a reputation as an "expert in Jewish affairs" and the SS, in general, to seize control of the Jewish policy.
November 9–10, 1938	During Kristallnacht (the Night of Broken Glass), thousands of Jewish homes, businesses, and synagogues are attacked in Germany and Austria. Around one hundred Jews are killed and many others beaten, while some twenty thousand Jewish men are marched off to concentration camps.
November 1938	The Kindertransport (children's transport) begins, allowing around ten thousand Jewish children to leave Germany over the next months.
July 1939	The T-4 program begins. It involves the intentional killing by state authorities of tens of thousands of Germany's mentally and physically disabled people. Some are killed in gas chambers.
September 1, 1939	Nazi Germany invades Poland, beginning World War II.

October 1939	Having defeated Poland, Nazi authorities—notably the SS—begin to enclose Poland's population of over three million Jews in ghettos.
1940	Germany defeats Norway, Denmark, the Netherlands, Belgium, Luxembourg, and France but fails to subdue Great Britain.
June 22, 1941	Nazi Germany launches a massive invasion of the Soviet Union.
July 1941	Special units of SS troops, known as Einsatzgruppen, begin massacres of Jewish civilians in areas of the Soviet Union recently taken by German forces. They also instigate pogroms and seek help among local non-Jewish civilians. These attack squads are under the leadership of SS General Reinhard Heydrich.
July 31, 1941	Heydrich receives a memorandum from Hermann Goering, Hitler's second in command, authorizing him to seek a "complete solution to the Jewish question" in Nazi-occupied Europe.
August–December, 1941	Seeking a more efficient form of killing than mass shootings, SS officials and the Einsatzgruppen experiment with mobile, so-called gas vans.
	SS officers connected with the T-4 program are transferred to Poland to assist in establishing killing operations there, notably at the Chelmno concentration camp.

Chronology

December 1941 The entrance of the United States into World War II, following Japan's attack on Pearl Harbor, as well as the failure of German forces to seize the Soviet capital of Moscow, convince Nazi leaders that World War II will be longer and harder than they had hoped, justifying for them extreme measures.

January 20, 1942 Heydrich, Eichmann, and other Nazi officials meet at the Wannsee Conference, the event generally understood as the point at which the mass murder of Jews became official German policy.

February–July, 1942 Six sites emerge as extermination and labor camps for Jews, all in or next to German-occupied Poland: Chelmno, Majdanek, Belzec, Sobibor, Treblinka, and Auschwitz. All are in operation by the summer of 1942.

May 1942 Heydrich is assassinated. Eichmann, supervised by SS chief Heinrich Himmler, remains the Holocaust's top administrator.

July 1942 The liquidation of the Warsaw Ghetto begins. Some Jews begin to plan for armed resistance.

December 1942 Having received some evidence of the massacres of Jews, leaders of the Allied nations issue a public declaration condemning the action and pledging to hold leaders responsible.

April–May 1943 The Warsaw Ghetto Uprising allows a small number of Jews to hold German forces at bay for several weeks.

November–December 1943	Three of the death camps—Belzec, Sobibor, and Treblinka—close, having accomplished their task of killing most remaining Jews in Poland. Jews continue to be sent to Auschwitz from southern and western Europe.
May–June 1944	During Auschwitz's Hoess Action, named for the former commandant at Auschwitz, Rudolf Hoess (who returned for the event), hundreds of thousands of Hungarian Jews are gassed.
July 22, 1944	The Majdanek death camp is liberated by Soviet forces.
November 1944	Himmler orders that gassings be stopped at all remaining camps and attempts to destroy facilities at Auschwitz.
January 1945	With Soviet forces approaching, the Germans abandon Auschwitz, forcing many surviving prisoners to retreat to Germany itself in the so-called Death Marches.
January–April 1945	Survivors of the Death Marches are dumped at Germany's concentration camps.
April 30, 1945	Hitler commits suicide.
May 7, 1945	Germany surrenders, ending World War II.
November 1945	The trials of twenty-one surviving top Nazis begin in the German city of Nuremburg. Among the charges is that of crimes against humanity such as the

	Holocaust. Eleven of them are eventually condemned to death for their crimes.
1948	The modern nation of Israel is founded, created largely by Jewish settlers and refugees from Europe.
1953	Israel establishes an annual Holocaust Remembrance Day.
1961	Eichmann, having been arrested after escaping to Argentina following World War II, is placed on trial in Israel. He is found guilty and condemned to death.
1993	The United States Holocaust Memorial Museum is opened in Washington, DC.

CHAPTER 1

The History of the Holocaust

Chapter Exercises

ESTIMATED JEWISH POPULATION OF EUROPE, 1939 AND 1946

Country	1939	1946	Percentage Change
Albania	200	300	50%
Austria	60,000	15,000	-75%
Belgium	90,000	33,000	-63%
Bulgaria	50,000	45,000	-10%
Czechoslovakia	315,000	65,000	-79%
Denmark	7,000	5,500	-21%
Finland	2,000	1,800	-10%
France	320,000	180,000	-44%
Germany	215,000	94,000	-56%
Greece	75,000	10,000	-87%
Holland	150,000	30,000	-80%
Hungary	400,000	200,000	-50%
Italy	50,000	46,000	-8%
Luxemburg	3,500	500	-86%
Norway	2,000	1,000	-50%
Poland	3,351,000	80,000	-98%
Rumania	850,000	335,000	-61%
Yugoslavia	75,000	11,000	-85%
United Kingdom	340,000	350,000	3%
Portugal	3,600	4,000	11%
Soviet Union	3,560,000	2,665,000	-25%
Spain	4,500	4,600	2%
Sweden	7,600	19,500	157%
Switzerland	26,000	28,600	10%
Total	**9,957,400**	**4,224,800**	**-58%**

Note: Data from 1946 US Department of State report. Some of the statistics may have been revised with later research.

Source: Anglo-American Committee of Inquiry, "Appendix III: Estimated Jewish Population of Europe," *Report to the United States Government and His Majesty's Government in the United Kingdom*, US Department of State, 1946.

1. **Analyzing Statistics**

    Question 1: Most of the Jewish victims of the Holocaust came from a few central and eastern European countries. What were those countries?

    Question 2: Which countries lost the largest percentage of their Jewish population during the Holocaust?

    Question 3: According to the chart, some nations had more Jewish people living in them in 1946 than in 1939. Why might that be?

2. **Writing Prompt**

    As if you were a journalist on the scene, write a "report from the field" covering the mass shooting operations that began the Holocaust. Come up with a clear title to grab your audience's attention, and include any background information needed to explain the events as well as important names, places, and ideas.

3. **Group Activity**

    Form into small groups and examine the central aspects of the Holocaust. Then, write a speech to such international organizations as the United Nations or the European Union making recommendations on how the outside world could respond to any nation or government that carries out such measures or threatens to.

VIEWPOINT 1

An Overview of the Holocaust
Christian Gerlach

In the 1940s, with World War II blazing, Nazi Germany and its dictator Adolf Hitler took steps to try to massacre Europe's Jewish population in what has come to be known as the Holocaust. In the following viewpoint, historian Christian Gerlach provides a broad description of the Holocaust. He touches on its origins in Nazi Germany's anti-Jewish policies in the 1930s as well as the broader context of anti-Semitism and dictatorship around Europe. He also describes how Nazi attitudes toward Jews and others resulted not only in massacre but slave labor and other atrocities. Christian Gerlach is professor of modern history at the University of Bern, Switzerland and the author of many articles and books on the Holocaust and genocide, including Extremely Violent Societies: Mass Violence in the 20th Century World.

The term *Holocaust* refers to the Nazi German policy that sought the annihilation of European and North African Jews. It comes from the Greek, *holókauton*, meaning "burnt sacrifice." More rarely, the term is also used to describe Nazi

---

Christian Gerlach, "Holocaust," *Encyclopedia of Genocide and Crimes Against Humanity*, vol. I, ed. Dinah L. Shelton. Farmington Hills, MI: Greenhaven Press, 2005, pp. 453–60. © 2005 Cengage Learning.

German violence in general. The persecution and mass murder of Europe's Jewry evolved out of a shift from religious to racial or ethnic anti-Semitism during the Industrial Revolution and the rise of liberal capitalism and the nation state in Europe during the second half of the nineteenth century. Prominent in many countries, including Russia and France, the new blend of anti-Semitism combined traditional and modern elements and became especially popular among many of Germany's intellectuals and elites. With the growing importance of the workers' movement and Marxism, anti-Semitism increased further after the Russian October revolution of 1917. Anti-Jewish conspiracy theories emerged, particularly in the states that lost World War I, that were established as its consequence, or that suffered badly in the worldwide economic crisis of 1929 to 1939. Most right-wing, authoritarian regimes that came to power in Europe in the 1920s and 1930s were anti-Semitic. Many adopted anti-Jewish laws. Chief among these, however, was Germany after Hitler's rise to power in 1933.

From 1933 to 1939, National Socialist (i.e., Nazi) Germany pursued a policy of enforced emigration. Out of 700,000 Jews in Germany and Austria, two-thirds left these countries before World War II, mostly the younger and more wealthy. Immigration restrictions abroad and Nazi "fees" for emigration permits hampered this process. Jews were dismissed from civil service in 1933. They faced economic ruin and the gradual expropriation of their property. They were routinely harassed, attacked by Nazi activists and youths, denied social services, and excluded from public education. Central as well as municipal institutions contributed to such policies. Sexual relations with non-Jews ("Aryans") were prohibited under the "Law for the Protection of the German Blood and Honor" in 1935. With the annexation of Austria in March 1938—where anti-Semitism was particularly widespread—and a nationwide pogrom ("Kristallnacht," or Crystal Night) on November 9 and 10, 1938, the persecution of Jews was intensified. Nearly 30,000 Jews were temporarily imprisoned in concentration camps after Kristallnacht, during which more than 1,000 synagogues were destroyed and Jewish shops were looted. At least 91 Jews died in the pogrom, and hundreds more committed suicide.

Beginning in late 1938, the influence of the SS and the police under Heinrich Himmler grew increasingly influential in setting Germany's anti-Jewish policy, although SS and police never gained exclusive control over it. After Germany successfully invaded Poland in September 1939, more than 2.5 million Polish Jews came under German rule. By May 1941, Germany occupied another eight European countries, further increasing this number. Anti-Semitic regulations aimed at the isolation, deprivation, and humiliation of Jews throughout Germany's vastly expanded territory were gradually adopted. Jews were forced to wear identifying insignia, their access to means of communication and transportation was limited, and their food rations were reduced. Local German authorities in Poland individually ordered the creation of Jewish ghettos wherein Jews were permitted extremely few resources and were assigned one room (or less) per family. The overcrowding led to increased mortality and the spread of diseases.

Beginning in 1939, German authorities developed plans for the enforced resettlement of the Jews to specially designated territories, where it was expected that harsh living conditions and an adverse climate would lead to their slow destruction. The first of these territories were eastern Poland, then Madagascar; later on, northern Russia or Siberia was considered. These plans called for the inmates to be separated according to sexes and kept under German "police supervision." Initially intended as postwar projects, these plans indicated a radicalization of anti-Semitic thinking under the Nazi regime. They were never implemented in their original form, but they fit into a larger framework of Nazi schemes for restructuring, ethnic cleansing, and resettlement in Eastern Europe. From 1939 to 1941, the SS tried to settle several hundred thousands of ethnic Germans from Eastern Europe in Western Poland. To make room for these newcomers, nearly 500,000 local inhabitants—including up to 200,000 Jews—were deported to the German-occupied General Government of Poland. Such actions increased the war-related scarcity of housing, sanitation, employment and food, particularly as a large proportion of the ethnic Germans had to stay in camps for months or years. The occupational authorities diverted the resulting shortages to the Jews and intensified the search for other "solutions."

Mass Murder of Soviet Jews

The German war against the Soviet Union was planned as a war of extermination jointly by Hitler, the SS, and military and economic authorities. The attack aimed at destroying "world communism," forcing "racially inferior" Slavs to submit to German colonial rule, eliminating the USSR as a military power, improving Germany's strategic position, and achieving self-sufficiency in food and raw materials such as oil. Schemes for large-scale German settlements had little influence on the actual occupation policy. While the majority of the Soviet population was to remain alive to provide cheap labor for the Germans, large groups of them were to be killed. Tens of millions were intended to die of starvation, particularly those who lived in the cities and the populations of certain northern and central areas. Also slated for death were millions of "commissars," communists, intellectuals, state officials, and Jews. This violence was considered vital for the long-term German appropriation of Soviet resources, which, in the short run, were needed for the militarily critical supplies of German troops fighting on the eastern front. The violence would also allow Germany to control a vast territory with a much smaller number of occupation troops than would otherwise be needed. Soviet Jews became a special target, because the racially charged propaganda blamed them for having designed the communist system, and they were expected to put up a fierce resistance.

Germany's military leaders wished to assign special units of the SS and the police the job of securing part of Soviet rear areas, thus reducing the need for using army troops to handle this task. These units included a total of 3,000 men in four *Einsatzgruppen* (Operation Units), deployed by the Security Police and Security Service under Reinhard Heydrich; mobile Police Battalions, deployed by the Order Police under Kurt Daluege; and Waffen-SS Brigades. These units started mass killings in the rear immediately after the German attack on June 22, 1941, and during that year more than 90 percent of their victims were Jewish.

The total extermination of Soviet Jews was not officially ordered at the outset. Instead, the SS and police targeted only those men considered to belong to the "Jewish intelligentsia": a group that included state officials, teachers, and lawyers, and others of the professional class. Between late July and early October 1941, this target group was enlarged—in different areas at different times—first by including women and children, and then by annihilating entire Jewish communities. This expansion began in Lithuania and Latvia, where the local, non-German, anti-Soviet police and administrators cooperated in acts of persecution and violence. By the end of 1941, 800,000 Jews had been killed throughout the German-occupied Soviet territories. Most victims were marched to remote locations near their home towns or cities and shot at previously prepared mass graves. . . .

Toward a Continent-Wide Program of Annihilation

The killing of the Soviet Jews marked the beginning of the extermination. Mass killings soon took place in other areas as well. Eastern Galicia had been declared part of the General Government, and was ruled under a German civil administration. By the end of 1941, 70,000 Jews from this region were killed. In Serbia, which was under military occupation, the German army killed the entire adult male Jewish population—7,000 in all—as reprisals against partisan resistance in the fall of 1941. The women and children were murdered by the SS and Police in 1942.

NAZI-CONTROLLED EUROPE

- Greater Germany and Occupied Territories
- German Allies or Dependent States
- Neutral
- Allies

Source: US Holocaust Museum, "German Administration of Europe 1942," www.ushmm.org.

In Poland, food rationing was intentionally unequal, with Jews receiving less than their non-Jewish fellow citizens, and much less than Germans. More than 40,000 Jews died of starvation and diseases related to overcrowding in the ghetto of Warsaw in 1941. In the German-annexed Reichsgau Wartheland (in Western Poland) and in the General Government, the civil administrations together with SS and the police developed plans for extermination camps to kill a portion of the Jewish population. The first killing center went into operation in Chelmno, Wartheland, on December 8, 1941, and the second was opened in Belzec, in the General Government's territory, on March 17, 1942.

It is unclear how much of this policy was ordered by the German central government and how much might have resulted from local initiatives. There were several parallel developments in German anti-Jewish policy in the fall of 1941, and Nazi leaders issued a number of declarations of intent (of which there remain only fragmented records). Beginning in mid-1941, experiments in new mass killing techniques, including gassing, were carried out by different branches of the SS and the police and in several concentration camps. Under pressure from the SS and regional Nazi Party leaders, Hitler permitted the deportation of Jews from the German Reich into the East in September 1941. By December, 50,000 had been deported to Lodz, Minsk, Kaunas, and Riga. Six thousand of these deportees were killed in Kaunas and Riga in late November 1941, after which Himmler called a temporary halt to the mass murders. However, they were resumed in Lodz and Minsk in May 1942.

Hitler announced his intention to exterminate all European Jews during World War II in a meeting of Nazi Party leaders on December 12, 1941, after declaring war on the United States. On January 20, 1942, in a high-level meeting in Berlin with government and Nazi Party officials plus SS officers, Heydrich claimed responsibility for "the solution to the Jewish question in Europe," and especially the definition of who was declared a "Jew" was discussed. He set out his plans for mass murder, which were probably still only vaguely developed at that time. In this meeting, called the Wannsee Conference, the governmental bureaucrats raised no objections to Heydrich's plans for the extermination of Europe's Jews, but they could not reach full agreement on how to proceed nor on a complete centralization of the measures against the Jews. Many scholars of the era argue that the extermination of European Jewry was ordered by Hitler no later than the autumn of 1941 (some saying that the order was issued early in the year), but others suggest that such a decision was not reached before December 1941 or in the spring of 1942. Some hold that the Holocaust simply "evolved," without the need for any explicit command decision issued by Hitler.

It has been argued that Himmler preferred using gas to kill Jews because he wanted to protect his firing squads in the east from mental stress. However, only a small proportion of the Soviet Jews were gassed in 1942 (in mobile gas vans). The majority, numbering some 500,000 in total, were shot. Killing techniques were never standardized. Only two of six major death camps (Auschwitz and Majdanek) employed prussic acid (also called Zyklon B) in gas chambers. In the Belzec, Sobibor, and Treblinka camps in the General Government, Jews were killed in stationary gas chambers into which engine exhaust fumes were vented. In Chelmno, the murders were performed in mobile gas vans. These killings differed from the mass murder of approximately 100,000 disabled patients. In that case, the patients were suffocated using bottled carbon monoxide, administered in stationary gas chambers or gas vans between September 1939 and August 1941. The killing of the disabled was organized by Hitler's chancellery in his capacity as the leader of the Nazi Party, known as the Kanzlei des Führers, or was carried out by regional civil administrations in annexed Western Poland, with the assistance of the SS. Personnel who had gained experience through participating in this "euthanasia" program (code named "T-4") were transferred to Belzec, Sobibor, and Treblinka in late 1941 and 1942.

Deportations

In Poland, the mass killings were expanded and accelerated in 1942 in two stages, similar to the way the policies were pursued in the German-occupied Soviet territories. General Governor Hans Frank argued that a policy of extermination could reduce food problems, health risks, and black market activities. Jews deemed unfit for work in the districts of Lublin, Galicia, and Krakow were deported on trains to Belzec, beginning on March 17, 1942 and to Sobibor beginning on May 6, 1942, while

The Holocaust

The bodies of thousands of slave laborers who were beaten and starved to death by the Nazis in Nordhausen, Germany, are prepared for burial in 1945. © John Florea/Time Life Pictures/Getty Images.

other victims were rounded up and killed in mass shootings. The second phase of the mass killings in the region began in July, with the establishment of a third death camp at Treblinka, near Warsaw. Construction on the camp had started in May, and murders began there on July 22, 1942. At the same time, new and bigger gas chambers were installed in Belzec, with Sobibor and Treblinka following suit during September and October of that year. On Himmler's orders (and with the support of the head of the German Four-Year Planning Office, Hermann Göring), the demand for forced labor was largely ignored during the period from July to October 1942, and many Jewish workers summarily killed. Approximately 1.15 million Jews from the General Government were thus killed in the second half of 1942, and only 297,000 remained alive.

The deportations of French and Slovakian Jews to Auschwitz began in March 1942, although most of the first deportees were not killed upon arrival. Auschwitz had been founded in 1940 as a concentration camp, but by 1942 it was gradually being transformed into a death center. Large-scale gassings began in early May 1942—the first victims were Jews from German-annexed East Upper Silesia in Poland—and the extermination of prisoners reached full scale in July 1942, handling transports of Jews arriving from Poland and Western and Central Europe. Between 10 and 35 percent of the new arrivals were selected for forced labor, the rest were killed. The first two permanent, if improvised, gas chambers in the main camp of Auschwitz went into operation in May and on June 30, 1942. Planning for bigger gas chambers and crematoria to be built in the subcamp of Auschwitz-Birkenau began in August, but they only became operational in March 1943. More than half of all the Jews who were killed in the Holocaust died between March 1942 and March 1943.

Massive transports of Jews from Western and Central Europe began to arrive in Auschwitz in June 1942. Deportations of Jews from the Netherlands progressed smoothly, but in Belgium and France the deportees were primarily, if not exclusively, limited to foreign Jews (the authorities in these two states were reluctant to cooperate in the deportation of their own citizens). Many Jews from Germany, particularly the elderly, were sent at first to a "show" camp in the Czech town of Terezín (Theresienstadt), allegedly as a place for convenient long-term settlement, but most were later sent to Auschwitz to be killed. Deportations to Auschwitz continued throughout 1943, and the later transports included Greek and (beginning in autumn, 1943) Italian Jews. To a certain extent, the definition of "Jew" was kept vague. Outside of the eastern territories, however, Jews married to gentiles and so-called half-Jews were usually not murdered, even though they were required to register. Some German officials, and Hitler himself, objected to killing Jews of mixed heritage because they were afraid of protests by non-Jewish relatives.

The extermination of European Jews reached a new peak in the summer of 1944, after Germany invaded Hungary, and the new (but not yet fully fascist) Hungarian government fully cooperated in the deportation of 430,000 Jews to Auschwitz in only seven weeks, from May 15 to July 9. About 100,000 of the Hungarian Jews were selected for forced labor—they were assigned to work in the construction of factories for German fighter planes and other tasks. Another 80,000 Jews were exempted from deportation and consigned instead to the Hungarian Army's forced Labor Service. Deportations were temporarily stopped by the Hungarian leader, Admiral Miklos Horthy, on July 9. He balked at transporting the more "useful" urban Jews of Budapest. After Horthy was ousted from office by the fascist Arrow-Cross Party on October 15, 1944, the transports were resumed on a limited scale. In total, nearly 500,000 of Hungary's approximately 730,000 Jews were killed.

Deportation transports from outside the General Government and the Soviet Union were organized by the office for Jewish affairs (IV B 4) in the Head Office of Reich Security under Adolf Eichmann. Because they usually deployed only several hundred men for each occupied country, the security police and security service required the cooperation of the German military and civil administrators, foreign office occupation personnel, the local national police and administrations, and German and foreign railway authorities. As a result, deportations were not only based on complex bureaucratic procedures but depended also on negotiations at a political level.

By the fall of 1943, virtually all remaining Jews in German-ruled Central and Eastern Europe had been interned within the concentration camp system of the SS. In 1944, Himmler gave orders not to let prisoners fall into enemy hands during military retreats. In the last months of World War II, this led to murderous death marches, in which columns of concentration camp inmates were forced to walk hundreds of kilometers, on often circuitous routes, with few supplies, and under brutal treatment by their guards, by German Nazi Party organizations, by home defense units, and by individuals. Estimates of the mortality in these marches range from less than a third to half of the participants. . . .

Consequences

Reliable statistics document that between 5.5 and 6.1 million Jews were killed in the Holocaust. Between 2.2 and 2.5 million of these deaths came from the Soviet Union, 1.9 million from Poland (both within the borders of 1945), 500,000 from "Greater Hungary" of 1944, 165,000 from Germany, 100,000 from the Netherlands, and 80,000 from France. Three million victims were killed by gassing, nearly two million were shot, the others were killed by other methods, died of starvation, exhaustion, forced labor, or the extreme living conditions imposed on them.

Among long-range consequences of the Holocaust was the loss of much of Europe's Jewish cultural heritage. This loss was further exacerbated by the postwar emigration of survivors to Israel and other countries. The Holocaust also led to the traumatization of generations of Europe's Jews, suffered not only by the survivors but also by many of their descendants. The Holocaust has been understood as an expression of a moral crisis either of European civilization, or the modern industrial society in general. Together with the enforced resettlements, population exchanges, and border adjustments during and after World War II, the Holocaust contributed to the emergence of ethnically and culturally far more homogeneous nation states after 1945.

Juridical trials and investigations against the perpetrators of the Holocaust took part in two phases, first during the immediate postwar era and then after 1957. Initially seen as one crime among others (there was no separate treatment of the Holocaust among the thirteen Nuremberg Trials), a special awareness developed over time, and was evident in cases like the Einsatzgruppen and Auschwitz trials in West Germany (1957–58, 1963) and the Eichmann trial in Israel in 1961. Although nearly 100,000 persons were under investigation for Nazi violence in the two German states, an equal number in the Soviet Union, and many in the rest of Europe, few (except in the USSR under Stalin) received substantial punishment, and the trials raised doubts as to whether legal systems can adequately respond to modern mass violence, given a general lack of documentation and the division of labor and state-level participation of the crime. However, the trials did succeed in educating the public, and in the accumulation and dissemination of knowledge about the Holocaust. Further, they provided the opportunity for symbolic atonement.

Viewpoint 2

A 1938 Pogrom Against German Jews Was an Important Step Toward the Holocaust

Anonymous

After Adolf Hitler and the Nazis took power in Germany in 1933, they began to implement anti-Semitic policies directed at the country's minority of about half a million Jews. These included a failed boycott of Jewish businesses in 1933, the ousting of Jews from civil service and media jobs, and, in 1935, the Nuremburg Laws. These removed German citizenship from Jews and banned intermarriage and sexual activity between Jews and non-Jews. As a result of these measures and the general atmosphere of intolerance, instances of random violence against Jewish people became fairly common, but it was not until 1938 that Hitler's government actively promoted violence against Jews, using state agencies like the police to carry it out.

The following viewpoint, from a website maintained by the United States Holocaust Memorial Museum, describes the most important example of this: the Kristallnacht pogroms, or anti-Jewish attacks, of November 1938. Then, Jewish homes, businesses, and synagogues were targeted by the SA, or Storm Troopers, as well as members of the increasingly influential Schutzstaffel (SS), a security service that attracted the most fanatical Nazis. Other officials simply looked on. In the aftermath of the attacks, and for

"Kristallnacht: A Nationwide Pogrom, November 9–10, 1938," *Holocaust Encyclopedia*, The United States Holocaust Memorial Museum, June 10, 2013. Copyright © 2013 by United States Holocaust Memorial Museum. All rights reserved. Reproduced by permission.

the first time, thousands of Jewish men were sent off to Hitler's concentration camps simply because they were Jewish.

Kristallnacht, literally, "Night of Crystal," is often referred to as the "Night of Broken Glass." The name refers to the wave of violent anti-Jewish pogroms which took place on November 9 and 10, 1938, throughout Germany, annexed Austria, and in areas of the Sudetenland in Czechoslovakia recently occupied by German troops.

Instigated primarily by Nazi Party officials and members of the SA (*Sturmabteilungen*: literally Assault Detachments, but commonly known as Storm Troopers) and Hitler Youth, *Kristallnacht* owes its name to the shards of shattered glass that lined German streets in the wake of the pogrom—broken glass from the windows of synagogues, homes, and Jewish-owned businesses plundered and destroyed during the violence.

In its aftermath, German officials announced that *Kristallnacht* had erupted as a spontaneous outburst of public sentiment in response to the assassination of Ernst vom Rath, a German embassy official stationed in Paris. Herschel Grynszpan, a 17-year-old Polish Jew, had shot the diplomat on November 7, 1938. A few days earlier, German authorities had expelled thousands of Jews of Polish citizenship living in Germany from the Reich; Grynszpan had received news that his parents, residents in Germany since 1911, were among them.

Initially denied entry into their native Poland, Grynszpan's parents and the other expelled Polish Jews found themselves stranded in a refugee camp near the town of Zbaszyn in the border region between Poland and Germany. Already living illegally in Paris himself, a desperate Grynszpan apparently sought revenge for his family's precarious circumstances by appearing at the German embassy and shooting the diplomatic official assigned to assist him.

Vom Rath died on November 9, 1938, two days after the shooting. The day happened to coincide with the anniversary of

Men walk by Jewish-owned businesses vandalized during Kristallnacht in November 1938. Homes and synagogues were also targeted for attack by the Nazis as part of the attack.
© Bettmann/Corbis/AP Images.

the 1923 Beer Hall Putsch, an important date in the National Socialist calendar. The Nazi Party leadership, assembled in Munich for the commemoration, chose to use the occasion as a pretext to launch a night of antisemitic excesses. Propaganda minister Joseph Goebbels, a chief instigator of the pogrom, intimated to the convened Nazi 'Old Guard' that 'World Jewry' had conspired to commit the assassination and announced that, "the Führer has decided that . . . demonstrations should not be prepared or organized by the Party, but insofar as they erupt spontaneously, they are not to be hampered."

Goebbels' words appear to have been taken as a command for unleashing the pogrom.

After his speech, the assembled regional Party leaders issued instructions to their local offices. Violence began to erupt in various parts of the Reich throughout the late evening and early morning hours of November 9–10. At 1:20 A.M. on November 10, Reinhard Heydrich, in his capacity as head of the Security Police (*Sicherheitspolizei*) sent an urgent telegram to headquarters and stations of the State Police and to SA leaders in their various districts, which contained directives regarding the riots. SA and Hitler Youth units throughout Germany and its annexed territories engaged in the destruction of Jewish-owned homes and businesses; members of many units wore civilian clothes to support the fiction that the disturbances were expressions of 'outraged public reaction.'

Despite the outward appearance of spontaneous violence, and the local cast which the pogrom took on in various regions throughout the Reich, the central orders Heydrich relayed gave specific instructions: the "spontaneous" rioters were to take no measures endangering non-Jewish German life or property; they were not to subject foreigners (even Jewish foreigners) to violence; and they were to remove all synagogue archives prior to vandalizing synagogues and other properties of the Jewish communities, and to transfer that archival material to the Security Service (*Sicherheitsdienst,* or SD). The orders also indicated that police officials should arrest as many Jews as local jails could hold, preferably young, healthy men.

The rioters destroyed 267 synagogues throughout Germany, Austria, and the Sudetenland [in Czechoslovakia]. Many synagogues burned throughout the night, in full view of the public and of local firefighters, who had received orders to intervene only to prevent flames from spreading to nearby buildings. SA and Hitler Youth members across the country shattered the shop windows of an estimated 7,500 Jewish-owned commercial establishments, and looted their wares. Jewish cemeteries became a particular object of desecration in many regions.

Destruction and Murder Reign

The pogrom proved especially destructive in Berlin and Vienna, home to the two largest Jewish communities in the German

Reich. Mobs of SA men roamed the streets, attacking Jews in their houses and forcing Jews they encountered to perform acts of public humiliation. Although murder did not figure in the central directives, *Kristallnacht* claimed the lives of at least 91 Jews between 9 and 10 November. Police records of the period document a high number of rapes and of suicides in the aftermath of the violence.

As the pogrom spread, units of the SS and Gestapo (Secret State Police), following Heydrich's instructions, arrested up to 30,000 Jewish males, and transferred most of them from local prisons to Dachau, Buchenwald, Sachsenhausen, and other concentration camps. Significantly, *Kristallnacht* marks the first instance in which the Nazi regime incarcerated Jews on a massive scale simply on the basis of their ethnicity. Hundreds died in the camps as a result of the brutal treatment they endured; most obtained release over the next three months on the condition that they begin the process of emigration from Germany. Indeed, the effects of *Kristallnacht* would serve as a spur to the emigration of Jews from Germany in the months to come.

In the immediate aftermath of the pogrom, many German leaders, like Hermann Göring, criticized the extensive material losses produced by the antisemitic riots, pointing out that if nothing were done to intervene, German insurance companies—not Jewish-owned businesses—would have to carry the costs of the damages. Nevertheless, Göring and other top Party leaders decided to use the opportunity to introduce measures to eliminate Jews and perceived Jewish influence from the German economic sphere. The German government made an immediate pronouncement that "the Jews" themselves were to blame for the pogrom and imposed a punitive fine of one billion *Reichsmark* (some 400 million US dollars at 1938 rates) on the German Jewish community. The Reich government confiscated all insurance payouts to Jews whose businesses and homes were looted or destroyed, leaving the Jewish owners personally responsible for the cost of all repairs.

The Nuremburg Laws

Nazi Germany's Nuremburg Laws were the first major anti-Semitic measures put in place by Adolf Hitler's government. Announced at the Nazi Party's annual rally in the southern German city of Nuremburg in September 1935, the two laws provided the foundation by which hundreds of thousands of Jewish people living in Germany had their rights steadily and systematically taken away.

The Reich Citizenship Law established that Jews in Germany could no longer be full citizens of the German state, and, therefore, should no longer necessarily expect such rights as police protection or the ability to get a passport. Nor could they vote or hold public office. In effect, German Jews were now stateless "subjects" rather than true citizens. The law furthermore established a legal definition for "Jewishness" based not on religion or cultural identification but on ancestry: one was a Jew if one had at least three Jewish grandparents.

The Law for the Protection of German Blood and Honor made it illegal for Jews to marry non-Jews. It also banned sexual activity between Jews and so-called "Aryan" Germans. Further provisions of the law made it a crime for Jews to display the German flag and for Germans to hire Jewish women under age forty-five as domestic servants.

With this legal foundation in place, other restrictive measures soon followed. Beginning in 1936, German Jews were forbidden, for example, from using state-run hospitals, from taking advantage of public facilities such as parks or playgrounds, and from being educated in state schools past the age of fourteen. By 1941, with World War II underway, remaining Jews in Germany were forced to wear a yellow Star of David armband in public.

A Turning Point Comes

In the weeks that followed, the German government promulgated dozens of laws and decrees designed to deprive Jews of their property and of their means of livelihood. Many of these laws enforced "Aryanization" policy—the transfer of Jewish-owned enterprises and property to "Aryan" ownership, usually for a fraction of their true value. Ensuing legislation barred Jews, already ineligible for employment in the public sector, from practicing most professions in the private sector, and made further strides in removing Jews from public life. German education officials expelled Jewish children still attending German schools. German Jews lost their right to hold a driver's license or own an automobile; legislation fixed restrictions on access to public transport. Jews could no longer gain admittance to "German" theaters, movie cinemas, or concert halls.

The events of *Kristallnacht* represented one of the most important turning points in National Socialist antisemitic policy. Historians have noted that after the pogrom, anti-Jewish policy was concentrated more and more concretely into the hands of the SS. Moreover, the passivity with which most German civilians responded to the violence signaled to the Nazi regime that the German public was prepared for more radical measures. The Nazi regime expanded and radicalized measures aimed at removing Jews entirely from German economic and social life in the forthcoming years, moving eventually towards policies of forced emigration, and finally towards the realization of a Germany "free of Jews" (*judenrein*) by deportation of the Jewish population "to the East."

Thus, *Kristallnacht* figures as an essential turning point in Nazi Germany's persecution of Jews, which culminated in the attempt to annihilate the European Jews.

VIEWPOINT 3

The Holocaust Began with Mass Shootings on the Eastern Front

Doris L. Bergen

In the following viewpoint, Holocaust scholar Doris L. Bergen examines how the mass murder of Jews began in the context of the Nazi invasion of the Soviet Union in June 1941. Already, Jews in Poland had been forced into ghettos and subjected to slave labor, while some Western European Jews were being sent to the Polish ghettos. But in the vast areas of the Soviet Union through which German armies were to pass—today parts of nations such as Lithuania, Latvia, Belarus, Ukraine, and Russia—there lived some five million Jews.

Bergen describes how the Nazi paramilitary organization Schutzstaffel (SS) formed special squads known as Einsatzgruppen to perform various brutal functions during the invasion, functions that eventually included mass shooting operations. In these, the Einsatzgruppen were assisted by the SS Order Police as well as, sometimes, local anti-Semites. Even elements of the regular German army, Bergen argues, were not entirely innocent. All in all, well over one million Jews as well as tens of thousands of others were killed in these shooting operations, which began before gassing

Doris L. Bergen, "War and Genocide: A Concise History of the Holocaust," *War and Genocide: A Concise History of the Holocaust*, 2nd ed. Lanham, MD: Rowman and Littlefield, 2009, pp. 153–59. Copyright © 2009 by Rowman and Littlefield. All rights reserved. Reproduced by permission.

facilities were built. Doris L. Bergen is Chancellor Rose and Ray Wolfe Professor of Holocaust Studies at the University of Toronto and the author of several books, including War and Genocide *and* The Holocaust: A New History.

From the beginning of war with the Soviet Union [June 22, 1941], the German leadership advocated unprecedented, ruthless measures. In instructions to the military and the SS, Hitler, Himmler, and Heydrich made it clear that no mercy was to be shown Germany's enemies, whether they were Jews, Communists, or resistors. High-ranking officers passed the message down to their men.

With the invasion of the Soviet Union the Nazi leadership would move to full implementation of their ideas of race and space on a massive scale. Their warfare reached new depths of brutality, especially against civilians but also against Soviet prisoners of war. Most noticeably they crossed the line from persecution and killing of Jews to a systematic attempt at total destruction.

Yet in many ways 1941 was not a radical break with earlier Nazi practices. All of the pieces were already in place. Hitler had spelled out the quest for Lebensraum in *Mein Kampf*. The Germans had begun to grab territory in Europe even before the war. They had assaulted civilians on a wide scale in Poland since 1939; they had used their enemies as slave labor, forcibly relocated enormous numbers of people, and started to slaughter Jews, Gypsies, and people deemed handicapped even before June 1941. In 1940 in France they had massacred thousands of captured black soldiers. All of these terrible developments culminated in the Soviet Union in 1941 and the years to follow.

Special Killing Squads Come into Being

Perhaps the most glaring sign of Germany's brutal style of warfare in 1941 was the use of special murder squads. German authorities dispatched mobile killing units to follow the regular military into

The Holocaust

Kindertransport

Jewish people steadily emigrated from Germany as their rights and opportunities were taken away from them by the Nazi government in the 1930s. But it was not until the Kristallnacht pogrom of November 1938 that other nations began to fully understand that German Jews were in grave danger and that special steps should be taken to help more of them escape. One such step was the transportation of children, known as Kindertransport, made available in the latter months of 1938 and much of 1939.

Kindertransport, or, more formally, Refugee Children's Movement, was first proposed by Jewish and Quaker groups in Great Britain to Britain's leaders in November 1938, shortly after Kristallnacht. After debating the matter, Britain's House of Commons agreed to waive immigration rules for Jewish (and a few Christian) children living under Nazi control. Conditions included finding homes where the children could be placed, as well as a guarantee of a particular amount of money for each child. The children's par-

---

Soviet territory. The main units, known as the *Einsatzgruppen*, "special action groups," included between five hundred and one thousand men each, many of them well educated, lawyers, theologians, and other professionals. The Einsatzgruppen worked together with more numerous German units known as the Order Police. Both the Einsatzgruppen and the Order Police cooperated with the German military.

The task of the mobile killing units was straightforward. They had explicit instructions from Heydrich to kill Jews, prominent Communists, and anyone suspected of sabotage or anti-German activity. Officially their goal was to combat Bolshevism and prevent guerrilla warfare. In fact, during the summer of 1941, they began to interpret their primary job as [the] slaughter of all Jews, including women, children, and old people. The Einsatzgruppen and Order Police also murdered Gypsies and inmates of men-

ents could not accompany them. Once the measure was approved, Jewish organizations quickly set about finding foster homes, ensuring the necessary funding, and sending representatives to Germany to select the children and arrange transport for them. At that point—happy to see more Jewish children emigrate—Nazi officials largely cooperated in the planning.

The first group of children to emigrate arrived in Great Britain on December 2, 1938. They travelled first by train to Holland, and then by boat to the British port city of Harwich. Most quickly went on to foster homes, whether Jewish or Christian, around Great Britain. This first transport was followed by many others until the effort became impossible with the start of World War II on September 1, 1939. Altogether around ten thousand children from not only Germany but German-controlled Austria and Czechoslovakia took part in the transports.

The vast majority of the Kindertransport children left behind parents who had to make the difficult decision to let them go. Although some of the children were able to reunite with their parents once the war was over, many others found that their parents died in the Holocaust.

---

tal hospitals, although they seem to have been less systematic against those target populations.

Members of the mobile killing units tried to involve local people in their work. Many non-German auxiliaries—Ukrainians, Latvians, ethnic Germans from Eastern Europe, Belorussians, and others—helped in their grisly task. Threats, bribes, massive amounts of alcohol, and promises of privileges for recruits and their families all helped the Germans find willing henchmen.

The Einsatzgruppen and Order Police attempted to stir up pogroms wherever they went. In some cases locals did take spontaneous action against Jews, but the mobile killing groups were less successful in this regard than they had hoped. Local individuals sometimes launched spontaneous attacks on Jews and took the initiative to steal their property, but generally the impetus and organization for systematic killing came from the Germans.

Witnesses to Massacre

Many of the actions of the mobile killing units more or less followed the same pattern. First they rounded up the Jews in a given area using various ruses to deceive them and relying on local collaborators for denunciations. The Germans ordered large pits dug in some convenient area—a local cemetery, nearby forest, or easily accessible field. Often they forced the prisoners themselves to dig what would be their own graves. At gunpoint they made the victims undress. Then they shot them by groups directly into the graves. In this manner the mobile killing units and their accomplices killed around a million people even before construction of killing centers for gassing had begun.

Of course, such mass killings in the open air could hardly be kept secret. Eyewitnesses of all kinds saw these shootings—German soldiers and workers, ethnic Germans who lived nearby, Russian, Polish, or Ukrainian families from the region, and others. Some of those observers gave detailed, chilling accounts of what they saw. For example, a German builder named Hermann Graebe watched while mobile killing squads shot scores of people of all ages near Dubno in Ukraine. He was surprised to be allowed to stay, but he noticed three uniformed postal workers looking on as well.

Elsewhere in Ukraine a fifteen-year-old Mennonite boy and his friends saw the slaughter of a group of Gypsies at a local cemetery. Later someone came around the village to distribute clothes taken from the murdered people. According to the eyewitness's account, no one in that particular Mennonite (and ethnic German) community wanted anything to do with booty won in such a way.

Most of our information about the mass shootings comes from the perpetrators themselves or from onlookers. Few victims lived to tell about their experiences. One of the exceptions is a man named Zvi Michalowsky, whose account appears in a book by Yaffa Eliach called *Hasidic Tales of the Holocaust*.

In 1941 on Rosh Hashanah, the Jewish new year, Germans and their local helpers murdered the Jews in a Lithuanian town called Eisysky. Michalowsky, a teenaged boy at the time, was among those forced to strip and wait at the edge of a grave for a bullet. A split second before the Germans fired, Zvi threw himself back into the pit. Miraculously he avoided serious injury.

For the rest of that day Zvi lay in the mass grave, feeling the bodies pile up on top of him. Only long after the shooting had stopped did he dare to climb out. He ran, naked and covered with blood, to the nearest house, but when he knocked, the terrified Polish Christians who lived there refused to let him in. Finally he approached an old woman. He told her he was Jesus Christ come down from the cross, and she opened the door to him. Zvi Michalowsky went on to found a Jewish resistance group in the woods of Lithuania. He survived the war.

Probably the biggest slaughter carried out by the Einsatzgruppen and their helpers was the massacre at Babi Yar. In just two days in September 1941, German mobile killing units and local collaborators shot more than thirty thousand Jews and an unknown number of other people at Babi Yar, a ravine on the outskirts of the Ukrainian city of Kiev. That act, just months after the invasion of the Soviet Union, destroyed the thriving Jewish community in Kiev and its surrounding area.

Babi Yar Becomes the Killing Field

Germans continued to use Babi Yar as a killing field throughout the occupation of Ukraine. Some estimates of the total number of people killed there are as high as one hundred thousand. The majority were Jews, although others targeted by the German occupiers were murdered at Babi Yar as well. That massacre has become emblematic of the vicious brutality of Nazi Germans in the Soviet Union generally and particularly in Ukraine.

In Soviet times state authorities put up a monument to the victims of Babi Yar. The plaque dedicated the memorial to the more than one hundred thousand Soviet citizens killed there.

An Einsatzgruppen soldier stands ready to shoot a man kneeling on the edge of a partially filled mass grave in Vinnitsa, Soviet Union, in 1942. © Universal History Archive/Getty Images.

Nowhere did it mention that most of those dead were murdered solely because they were Jews. Here the official act of remembering also became a way of forgetting.

The exact number of people killed by the mobile units cannot be known, although German records have allowed experts in the field to come to an estimate approaching 2 million total victims. Most were Jews—some 1.3 million—and there may have been as many as 250,000 Gypsies. The Einsatzgruppen and Order Police followed the regular military and in many cases even relied on them for provisions, security, and intelligence. They could not have carried out such an enormous number of killings without the knowledge and cooperation of the Wehrmacht. How did the military respond?

Involvement of the Regular German Army

At first it seems there might have been some misgivings. One incident illustrates the forms such doubts might have taken. In mid-August 1941, German authorities in the Ukrainian town of Belaya Tserkov, more than two hundred miles east of Lvov, ordered local Jews to report for registration. Over the next few days, SS and German soldiers scoured the area for Jews, slaughtering hundreds of men and women.

In the summer of 1941 some of the killers still seemed unclear as to whether their task included murder of Jewish women and children as well as men. Perhaps for this reason, the shooters at Belaya Tserkov did not initially kill all the children. Instead they dumped about ninety of them and a handful of women in a school.

German soldiers in a field hospital nearby heard babies crying in the night. Uncertain how to respond, they appealed to their military chaplains. The two German clergy, a Protestant pastor and a Catholic priest, went to see for themselves. They were appalled. It was hot, but the children were crammed into a small space without water, food, or adult care. Some of the mothers were locked in an adjoining room, from which they could see the misery of their children without being able to get to them.

The Holocaust

The chaplains appealed to the local military commander, an elderly Austrian, to take pity on the children. Their effort failed, one of them later reported, because the man was a convinced antisemite. Together the chaplains convinced another German officer to intervene. He got Army High Command to agree to postpone shooting of the children, but SS representatives and military officers on the spot prevailed, pointing to instructions from General Field Marshal Gerd von Runstedt, commander of Army Group South, that they were to show no mercy.

On 21 August 1941, the children were taken from the school and killed. It is unclear whether it was Germans or Ukrainian volunteers who did the job.

Killings of civilians did not end in the summer or fall of 1941 but continued throughout the war. Presumably German soldiers and the military chaplains who ministered to them got used to the routine. The comfort of knowing they were backed by orders from above must have helped too.

One of the most widely circulated of such orders came in October 1941 from German Field Marshal Walter von Reichenau. Reichenau admitted that there was "uncertainty" among the German troops as to the current situation in the east. However, he told his men, given the nature of this war and the need to destroy what he called the "Jewish-Bolshevist system" completely, it was necessary to break the conventional rules of war, to show no mercy to those defined as Germany's enemies, above all the people Reichenau labeled "Jewish subhumans."

It is certainly not common practice for military superiors to justify themselves and their decisions to their men. Reichenau, however, did just that. His order implies that there was some uneasiness in the ranks about military involvement in [the] slaughter of civilians. We can assume that those reservations were overcome. After all, the killings continued with the necessary military support. Perhaps German soldiers accepted the official justifications offered to them, that such excesses were a necessary part of the German struggle against partisans, or later on, that they were some kind of revenge for Allied bombings of German cities.

Of course neither of those rationalizations actually makes sense. How could a baby be responsible for a partisan attack on German rail lines? What could an old Jewish woman more than a thousand miles away who spoke nothing but Yiddish possibly have to do with British planes dropping bombs on Hamburg or Cologne? Nevertheless these nonsensical explanations may have helped men live with themselves once they were already involved in killing. Many of their motivations for killing in the first place were undramatic. Their comrades were doing it, and they did not want to stand out; they considered it part of their job; they had gotten used to it.

What we do know is that Germans were not forced to be killers. Those who refused to participate were given other assignments or transferred. To this day no one has ever found a single example of a German who was executed for refusing to take part in the killing of Jews or other civilians. Defense attorneys of Germans accused of war crimes during World War II have looked hard for such a case because it would support the claim that their clients were forced to kill. The Nazi system, however, did not work that way. There were enough willing perpetrators. For the most part coercive violence could be reserved for those deemed enemies.

VIEWPOINT 4

German Officials Discuss the "Final Solution to the Jewish Question"

Wannsee Protocol and Adolf Eichmann

On January 20, 1942, thirteen top officials of the Nazi Party, the German government, and the Schutzstaffel (SS) met for an important meeting in Wannsee, a wealthy Berlin suburb. Reinhard Heydrich, the second in command in the SS, chaired the meeting. The following viewpoint consists of a part of the official record of the meeting, the so-called Wannsee Protocol. In it, Heydrich makes it known that he has been tasked by his superiors to seek a "final solution to the Jewish problem in Europe." The basis of that solution was to be "evacuation," a euphemism that those at the meeting came to understand meant mass killing. The Wannsee Protocol was edited by SS Colonel Adolf Eichmann who assembled it from a stenographer's notes. Although all copies of it were ordered destroyed, a single copy survived to be later discovered by US Army intelligence. Eichmann went on to be the chief administrator of the Holocaust following Heydrich's assassination in the spring of 1942.

II. At the beginning of the discussion SS-Obergruppenfuehrer [Reinhard] HEYDRICH gave information that the Reich

Copyright © 1982 from *The Holocaust: Selected Documents in Eighteen Volumes*, vol. 11 by Adolf Eichmann, ed. John Mendelsohn. Reproduced by permission of Taylor and Francis Group, LLC, a division of Informa plc.

Marshal [Hermann Goering] had appointed him delegate for the preparations for the final solution of the Jewish problem in Europe and pointed out that this discussion had been called for the purpose of clarifying fundamental questions. The wish of the Reich Marshal to have a draft sent to him concerning organisatory, factual and material interests in relation to the final solution of the Jewish problem in Europe, makes necessary an initial common action of all Central Offices immediately concerned with these questions in order to bring their general activities into line.

He said that the Reich Fuehrer-SS [Heinrich Himmler] and the Chief of the German Police (Chief of the Security Police and the SD [SS Security Office]) [Heydrich] was entrusted with the official handling of the final solution of the Jewish problem centrally without regard to geographic borders.

The Chief of the Security Police and the SD then gave a short report of the struggle which has been carried on against this enemy, the essential points being the following:

a) the expulsion of the Jews from every particular sphere of life of the German people,
b) the expulsion of the Jews from the Lebensraum [living space] of the German people.

In carrying out these efforts, an increased and planned acceleration of the emigration of Jews from the Reich territory was started, as the only possible present solution.

By order of the Reich Marshal a Reich Central Office for Jewish emigration was set up in January 1939 and the Chief of the Security Police and SD was entrusted with the management. Its most important tasks were

a) to *make* all necessary arrangements for the *preparation* for an increased emigration of the Jews,
b) to *direct* the flow of immigration,

c) to hurry up the procedure of emigration in each *individual* case.

The aim of all this being that of clearing the German Lebensraum of Jews in a legal way.

All the Offices realized the drawbacks of such enforced accelerated emigration. For the time being they had, however, tolerated it on account of the lack of other possible solutions of the problem.

The work concerned with emigration was, later on, not only a German problem, but also a problem with which the authorities of the countries to which the flow of emigrants was being directed would have to deal. Financial difficulties, such as the demand for increasing sums of money to be presented at the time of the landing on the part of various foreign governments, lack of shipping space, increasing restriction of entry permits, or canceling of such, extraordinarily increased the difficulties of emigration. In spite of these difficulties 537 000 Jews were sent out of the country between the day of the seizure of power and the deadline 31 October 1941. Of these as from 30 January from Germany proper approx. 360.000

from 15 March 1938 from Austria appr. 147.000

from 15 March 1939 from the Protectorate, Bohemia and Moravia appr. 30.000.

The Jews themselves, or rather their Jewish political organizations financed the emigration. In order to avoid the possibility of the impoverished Jews staying behind, action was taken to make the wealthy Jews finance the evacuation of the needy Jews, this was arranged by imposing a suitable tax, i.e. an emigration tax which was used for the financial arrangements in connection with the emigration of poor Jews, and was worked according to a ladder system.

Apart from the necessary Reichmark-exchange, foreign currency had to be presented at the time of the landing. In order to save foreign exchange held by Germany, the Jewish financial establishments in foreign countries were—with the help of Jewish organizations in Germany—made responsible for arranging for an adequate amount of foreign currency. Up to 30 October 1941, the foreign Jews donated approx. $9,500,000.

In the meantime the Reich Fuehrer-SS and Chief of the German Police had prohibited emigration of Jews for reasons of the dangers of an emigration during war-time and consideration of the possibilities in the East.

III. Another possible solution of the problem has now taken the place of emigration, i.e. the evacuation of the Jews to the East, provided the Fuehrer agrees to this plan.

Such activities are, however, to be considered as provisional actions, but practical experience is already being collected which is of greatest importance in relation to the future final solution of the Jewish problem.

Approx. 11,000,000 Jews will be involved in this final solution of the European problem. They are distributed as follows among the countries [see table].

The number of Jews given here for foreign countries includes, however, only those Jews who still adhere to the Jewish faith as the definition of the term "Jew" according to racial principles is still partially missing there. The handling of the problem in the individual countries will meet with difficulties due to the attitude end conception of the people there, especially in Hungary and Rumania. Thus, even today a Jew can buy documents in Hungary which will officially prove his foreign citizenship.

The influence of the Jews in all walks of life in the USSR is well known. Approximately 5 million Jews are living in the European Russia, and in Asiatic Russia scarcely ¼ million....

Under proper guidance the Jews are now to be allocated for labor to the East in the course of the final solution. Able-bodied Jews will be taken in large labor columns to these districts for work on roads, separated according to sexes, in the course of which action a great part will undoubtedly be eliminated by natural causes.

DISTRIBUTION OF JEWS TO BE INVOLVED IN THE FINAL SOLUTION

Country	Number	Country	Number
A		Finland	2,300
Germany proper	131,800	Ireland	4,000
Austria	43,700	Italy including Sardinia	58,000
Eastern territories	420,000	Albania	200
General Government	2,284,000	Croatia	40,000
Bialystok	400,000	Portugal	3,000
Protectorate Bohemia and Moravia	74,200	Rumania including Bessarabia	342,000
Estonia	free of Jews	Sweden	8,000
Latvia	3,500	Switzerland	18,000
Lithuania	34,000	Serbia	10,000
Belgium	43,000	Slovakia	88,000
Denmark	5,600	Spain	6,000
France		Turkey (European Turkey)	55,500
occupied territory	165,000		
unoccupied territory	700,000		
Greece	69,600	Hungary	742,800
Netherlands	160,800	USSR	5,000,000
Norway	1,300	Ukraine	2,994,684
		White Russia with exception of Bialystok	446,484
B			
Bulgaria	48,000		
England	330,000	**Total: over 11,000,000**	

"Evacuation" for "Labor"

The possible final remnant will, as it must undoubtedly consist of the toughest, have to be treated accordingly, as it is the product of natural selection, and would, if liberated, act as a bud cell of a Jewish reconstruction (see historical experience).

In the course of the practical execution of this final settlement of the problem, Europe will be cleaned up from the West to the East. Germany proper, including the protectorate Bohemia and Moravia, will have to be handled first because of reasons of housing and other social-political necessities.

The evacuated Jews will first be sent, group by group, into so-called transit-ghettos from which they will be taken to the East.

SS-Obergruppenfuehrer HEYDRICH went on to say that an important provision for the evacuation as such is the exact definition of the group of persons concerned in the matter.

It is intended not to evacuate Jews of more than 65 years of age but to send them to an old-age-ghetto—Theresienstadt [in Czechoslovakia] is being considered for this purpose.

Next to these age-groups—of the 280,000 Jews still in Germany proper and Austria on 31 October 1941, approximately 30% are over 65; Jews disabled on active duty and Jews with war decorations (Iron Cross I) will be accepted in the Jewish old-age-ghettos.

Through such expedient solution the numerous interventions will be eliminated with one blow.

The carrying out of each single evacuation project of a larger extent will start at a time to be determined chiefly by the military development. Regarding the handling of the final solution in the European territories occupied and influenced by us it was suggested that the competent officials of the Foreign Office working on these questions confer with the competent "Referenten" from the Security Police and the SD [SS Security Office].

In Slovakia and Croatia the difficulties arising from this question have been considerably reduced, as the most essential problems in this field have already been brought near to a solution. In Rumania the Government in the meantime has also appointed a commissioner for Jewish questions. In order to settle the question in Hungary it is imperative that an adviser in Jewish

The SS

The Holocaust was largely organized and carried out by officials and units of Nazi Germany's SS, a paramilitary wing of the Nazi Party. SS stands for the German word "Schutzstaffel," which can be translated as "protection squad" or, sometimes, "elite guard." Begun in the 1920s before Adolf Hitler took power, the SS was initially intended to provide security for top officials. But under the leadership of Heinrich Himmler, the SS became, by most standards, the most powerful organization within the Nazi state.

Himmler, a true believer in Nazi ideology and German racial superiority, became the head of the SS in 1929. His ambitions included turning the SS not only into a powerful organization but a reflection of what he perceived as the best of German characteristics. He recruited the well educated as well as aristocrats and military veterans. Those who joined the SS received careful training in ideology and obedience, and they had to fulfill strict physical requirements. These included proving that their blood was fully "German." Among those he recruited was a young former naval officer named Reinhard Heydrich, who eventually rose to be the No. 2 man in the organization.

After the Nazis took power in 1933, the power of the SS expanded rapidly. Himmler seized control of most of the police functions of Nazi Germany, including the management of the infamous Gestapo, or Secret State Police. The SS ran the concentration camps. Himmler, now holding the title of Reichsfuehrer-SS, also built up a fully militarized Waffen-SS, which was, in effect, a second German army.

questions be pressed upon the Hungarian government without too much delay.

As regards the taking of preparatory steps to settle the question in Italy SS-Obergruppenfuehrer HEYDRICH considers it opportune to contact the chief of the police with a view to these problems.

In 1938, a low-ranking SS officer named Adolf Eichmann opened the first SS Office for Jewish Emigration, which helped Jews to leave German territory provided they signed over most of their property and fulfilled other strict requirements. Eichmann's efforts helped to give the SS control over what Nazis called the "Jewish Question," bringing him to the attention of Himmler and Heydrich.

Following the Nazi conquest of Poland, the SS played the leading role in implementing occupation policies based on racial beliefs. These included establishing Jewish ghettos and organizing both Jews and Poles into slave labor battalions. Heydrich, from his new base of power as the governor of Nazi-occupied Czechoslovakia, was emerging as the most influential Nazi leader on the ground in occupied Eastern Europe.

SS troops effectively began the Holocaust with mass shooting operations, as part of the Nazi invasion of the Soviet Union in the summer of 1941. Meanwhile, Heydrich, who had organized the shooting squads, was authorized by Hermann Goering, Hitler's designated successor, to find and implement a "complete solution to the Jewish question." Eventually gassing was selected, and when Heydrich announced the measures to top Nazi bureaucrats at the Wannsee Conference of January 20, 1942, he left no doubt that the SS was in charge.

Heydrich was assassinated in the spring of 1942, but Adolf Eichmann, by then a self-proclaimed "expert in Jewish affairs," was ready to administer the Holocaust under Heinrich Himmler's guidance. Their crimes, as well as innumerable others, led the SS to be declared a criminal organization in 1945 by the victorious Allies—with all members to be arrested.

In the occupied and unoccupied parts of France the registration of the Jews for evacuation can in all probability be expected to take place without great difficulties.

Assistant Under Secretary of State [Martin] LUTHER in this connection calls attention to the fact that in some countries, such as the Scandinavian states, difficulties will arise if these problems are [not] dealt with thoroughly and that it will be therefore advisable to defer action in these countries. Besides, considering the small numbers of Jews to be evacuated from these countries this deferment means not essential limitation.

On the other hand, the Foreign Office anticipates no great difficulties as far as the South-East and the West of Europe are concerned.

Viewpoint 5

The Holocaust Just Got More Shocking
Eric Lichtblau

Most of the victims of the Holocaust died in one of six dedicated extermination camps specially designed or modified for the purpose. These six camps—Chelmno, Belzec, Sobibor, Treblinka, Majdanek, and Auschwitz—were all located in or near German-occupied Poland. In the following viewpoint, a journalist contends that these six camps were just a small part of a huge network of facilities maintained by Nazi Germany to take advantage of slave labor, punish opponents, and indeed, murder those deemed to be undesirable. Eric Lichtblau is a reporter for the New York Times *and a visiting fellow at the United States Holocaust Memorial Museum.*

Thirteen years ago [in 2000], researchers at the United States Holocaust Memorial Museum began the grim task of documenting all the ghettos, slave labour sites, concentration camps and killing factories that the Nazis set up throughout Europe.

Eric Lichtblau, "The Holocaust Just Got More Shocking," *New York Times*, March 9, 2013. © 2013 The New York Times. All rights reserved. Used by permission and protected by the copyright laws of the United States. The printing, copying, redistribution, or retransmission of this content without express written permission is prohibited.

The Holocaust

Ghettos

On September 21, 1939, Reinhard Heydrich, head of the Reich Security Main Office (RSHA) in the SS, sent the Schnellbrief, a directive that laid out the procedures and treatment towards the Jews in the areas of occupied Poland. It declared that Jews living in towns and villages would be transferred to join larger populations of Jews in the bigger cities, and that Jewish councils, known as "Judenräte," should be established, whose purpose was to carry out the orders of the German authorities. The Schnellbrief also set the Aryanization of Jewish factories as a goal, taking into consideration the needs of the German military and the economic importance of the factories. The Jews were generally housed in the poorest neighborhoods, and these areas were eventually turned into sealed ghettos, in which the majority of Polish Jewry was incarcerated. A large, hermetically sealed ghetto was established in Lodz in the spring of 1940, and in the autumn of 1940, the largest of the ghettos was established in Warsaw, where nearly half a million Jews were interned.

After the initial mass killings in the Soviet areas occupied by

What they have found so far has shocked even scholars steeped in the history of the Holocaust.

The researchers have catalogued about 42,500 Nazi ghettos and camps throughout Europe, spanning German-controlled areas from France to Russia and Germany itself, during Hitler's brutal reign from 1933 to 1945.

The figure is so staggering that even fellow Holocaust scholars had to make sure they had heard it correctly when the lead researchers previewed their findings at an academic forum in late January at the German Historical Institute in Washington.

The numbers are so much higher than we originally thought, institute director Hartmut Berghoff said after learning of the new data. We knew before how horrible life in the camps and ghettos was, but the numbers are unbelievable.

> the Germans beginning in June 1941, ghettos were established in these regions as well, even though the Germans intended to leave the Jews in these ghettos for a short time only before murdering them. The largest of these ghettos was established in Minsk, Belorussia, which held approximately 100,000 Jews. The Germans occupied Hungary in March 1944. In May they began deporting Hungarian Jewry to Auschwitz, and in November decreed the establishment of a ghetto in Budapest in which approximately 70,000 Jews from the city were imprisoned. In all, the Germans established more than 1,000 ghettos in Eastern Europe and a few ghettos in central and Southern Europe.
>
> The German authorities attained several goals by establishing the ghettos: they gathered large numbers of Jews together under conditions of severe congestion and close supervision, deprived them of their property, exploited their labor, isolated them from the rest of the world, made them vulnerable and unprepared at crucial moments, and incited the local population against the Jews, whom they resented anyway.
>
> *"The Holocaust: The Ghettos," Yad Vashem.*
> *www.yadvashem.org.*

The documented camps include not only killing centres but thousands of forced labour camps, where prisoners made war supplies; prisoner-of-war camps; sites euphemistically named care centres, where pregnant women were forced to have abortions or their babies were killed after birth; and brothels, where women were forced to have sex with German military personnel.

Auschwitz and a handful of other concentration camps have come to symbolise the Nazi killing machine in the public consciousness. Likewise, the Nazi system for imprisoning Jewish families in home-town ghettos has become associated with a single site the Warsaw Ghetto, known for the 1943 uprising. But the new research shows that these sites, infamous though they are, represent only a minuscule fraction of the German network. The maps the researchers have created to identify the camps and

The Holocaust

Slave laborers lie in their stacked bunks in a barrack at the Buchenwald concentration camp near Weimar, Germany, in April 1945. © Courtesy of the National Archives/Newsmakers/Getty Images.

ghettos turn wide sections of wartime Europe into black clusters of death, torture and slavery centred in Germany and Poland, but reaching in all directions. The lead editors on the project, Geoffrey Megargee and Martin Dean, estimate that 15 million to 20 million people died or were imprisoned in the sites that they have identified as part of a multi-volume encyclopaedia.

The existence of many individual camps and ghettos was previously known only on a fragmented, region-by-region basis. But the researchers, using data from 400 contributors, have documented the scale for the first time, studying where they were located, how they were run and what their purpose was.

The brutal experience of Henry Greenbaum, an 84-year-old Holocaust survivor who lives outside Washington, typifies the wide range of Nazi sites. By the age of 17, Mr Greenbaum had been enslaved in five camps in five years, and was on his way to a sixth, when US soldiers freed him in 1945. Nobody even knows about these places, Mr Greenbaum said. Everything should be documented. We try to tell the youngsters so that they know, and they'll remember. When the research began in 2000, Mr Megargee said he expected to find perhaps 7,000 Nazi camps and ghettos, based on postwar estimates. But the numbers kept climbing first to 11,500, then 20,000, then 30,000 and now 42,500. The numbers astound: 30,000 slave labour camps; 1,150 Jewish ghettos; 980 concentration camps; 1,000 prisoner-of-war camps; 500 brothels filled with sex slaves; and thousands of other camps used for killing the elderly and infirm, performing forced abortions, Germanising prisoners or transporting victims to killing centres. Co-researcher Mr Dean said the findings left no doubt that many Germans despite the frequent claims of ignorance after the war, must have known about the widespread existence of the Nazi camps at the time.

Viewpoint 6

Modern Students Visit One of the Death Camps of the Holocaust

Will Oliphant

In the following viewpoint, British journalist Will Oliphant reports on a visit to the Auschwitz death camp made by a group of teenaged students in 2009. Auschwitz was by far the largest of the death camps, with facilities ranging from gas chambers to factories and barracks for thousands of slave workers. Much of the camp still stands. Even though Nazi officials made vain attempts to destroy it in late 1944, as Germany was losing World War II, Auschwitz was simply too big to erase from the land. Oliphant quotes several students who were shocked and silenced by what they saw and heard from guides during the visit. As he notes, it was "no ordinary school trip." Will Oliphant writes for the Birmingham Mail, *the* Daily Mail, *and other United Kingdom newspapers.*

More than 60 years after the end of the Second World War, I'm standing on the train platform at Birkenau [at Auschwitz] wondering how it could have been allowed to happen.

It's very easy to look at the Holocaust as a page in history and to think of Auschwitz as just a word, especially when you're sitting at home watching a documentary on the television.

Will Oliphant, "A Horror We Cannot Forget," *Birmingham Mail*, March 19, 2009. Copyright © 2009 by Birmingham Post and Mail. All rights reserved. Reproduced by permission.

Then you suddenly realise you're standing at the station where 1.2 million Jews, gypsys, gay people, Russians, political prisoners and other Nazi non-desirables spilled dazed and confused into the light.

With the flick of an SS [Schutzstaffel] officer's hand, they were either condemned to immediate death in the gas chamber or sent to the horror of the labour camps.

That's why the Holocaust Education Trust [of the United Kingdom] has brought me here along with 200 sixth form students [the rough equivalent of high-school seniors] from around the West Midlands. The message is very simple, we must never forget the enormity of the atrocity.

That fact was brought home to us all very early in the day-long trip to the death camps when we visited the nearby town of Oswiecim. An educator from the trust asks students why they think the gates of a Jewish cemetery there would be locked.

The answer. Vandalism? No. Remaining prejudice? No.

There's simply no-one left to visit the graves. The last Jewish man to live here, a survivor of the holocaust, died here in 2000. The local Jewish population were either eradicated or didn't want to return.

At Auschwitz students walk under the entrance bearing the sign *Arbeit Macht Frei*, which means work will make you free, before being taken on guided tours of the barracks where the prisoners were kept.

Here we're shown items stripped from prisoners. Piles of glasses, suitcases and mountains of human hair cruelly shaved from the heads of prisoners by the Nazis and used to make clothes and fabric.

But despite these shocking sights, for me it wasn't until we got to Birkenau, the overflow camp for Auschwitz, that the reality of the place hits home.

The desolate landscape with endless ruins of huts and sheds used to keep the mainly Jewish population is both humbling and chokingly sad.

NAZI DEATH AND CONCENTRATION CAMPS

Map showing locations of Nazi death and concentration camps across Germany, Poland, and surrounding countries, including: Neuengamme, Stutthof, Ravensbrück, Bergen-Belsen, Sachsenhausen, Chelmno, Treblinka, Sobibor, Vught, Gross-Rosen, Majdanek, Buchenwald, Theresienstadt, Auschwitz-Birkenau, Bełżec, Natzweiler, Flossenburg, Mauthausen, Dachau.

Legend: Death camps / Concentration camps

Students around me are obviously affected as soon as we arrive at the place. People talk in hushed voices despite being out in the open.

Alex Taylor, from King Edward Camp Hill School for Boys, said: "I feel quite drained. Some of the things we've seen have been stomach turning. It brings it so much closer to you when you're here seeing it.

"It's hard to understand how human beings could have done this to each other. It [reinforced] what I had thought about the place. But you can't really appreciate it fully until you've been here."

Fellow King Edward student Vicky James added: "It was different to what I expected. It was really upsetting. It gave me a whole new insight into what the people and particularly the Jewish people suffered here.

"Walking through Birkenau, looking at the train tracks, seeing the buildings and seeing the guard tower which is so familiar at the end of the camp can't help but make you emotional."

As dusk falls the students are brought to a memorial site between the crematoriums where above the gas chambers the bodies of victims murdered here were burned.

Rabbi Barry Marcus—one of the men behind the trust's plans to bring students to Auschwitz—reads a prayer in Hebrew over a hushed crowd of students. This is no ordinary school trip.

He adds a final thought for people to take away with them.

"If we were to have a moment's silence for every person who died here during the holocaust, [we] would have to be silent for four years."

It recently came out in a survey that many British schoolchildren thought that Auschwitz was the name of a religious festival, a country or even a beer.

For these students the word Auschwitz will forever bring home memories of this day.

Viewpoint 7

Special Efforts Have Been Made in Both Israel and the United States to Keep the Memory of the Holocaust Alive

Norman J.W. Goda

In the following viewpoint, historian Norman J.W. Goda touches on attempts to memorialize the Holocaust. In the nation of Israel, which was itself founded in the aftermath of the Holocaust by, partly, Jewish refugees and survivors, Holocaust memory is especially important. National holidays, monuments, and even a large organization known as Yad Vashem work to not only commemorate the event but also to provide research and education. Meanwhile, the United States Holocaust Memorial Museum, opened in Washington, DC, performs similar functions in America. It has since been joined by other institutions such as the Museum of Tolerance in Los Angeles and the Shoah Foundation, based at the University of Southern California. Norman J.W. Goda is professor of Holocaust studies at the University of Florida and the author of Tomorrow the World: Hitler, Northwest Africa, and the Path Toward America; Tales from Spandau: Nazi Criminals and the Cold War, *and other books and articles on the Holocaust, Nazi Germany, and World War II.*

For better or worse, Israel's identity is closely linked with the Holocaust. Israeli memorialization initially aimed to stress,

Norman J.W. Goda, *The Holocaust: Europe, The World, and the Jews, 1918–1945,* Upper Saddle River, NJ: Pearson Education, 2013. © 2013. Reprinted by permission of Pearson Education, Inc.

amid the unimaginable loss, heroic Jewish resistance and the danger of weakness. The emphasis was based on the perception among many Zionists that historic Jewish passivity in the Diaspora [the dispersal of Jews from Jerusalem beginning in 71 AD] contributed to catastrophe. "Complacency," said historian Benzion Dinur, "plays a role in the destruction." With the new country surrounded by hostile Arab states, the legacy of the armed Jewish fighter rather than the Diaspora Jew had to form the national narrative even amid sorrow over the unarmed victims.

Israel's initial national memorial came in the form of Holocaust Remembrance Day (*Yom Ha'Shoah*), which emerged by act of the Israeli Knesset [parliament] in 1951. It is based on the recognition that, while nothing can replace individual religious mourning, collective, secular remembrance is also essential. Starting in 1958, official state ceremonies were held in Jerusalem, and after 1959, the entire state observed two minutes' silence. Even traffic comes to a stop. But the date, the 27th of Nissan, is significant. It coincides with the Warsaw ghetto uprising and sits between Passover, which commemorates the exodus from Egypt, and Israel's Day of Independence. The date thus honors ghetto fighters while linking them to the hard-won state. Ceremonies have connected ghetto fighters to contemporary Israeli soldiers while imploring Jews never to be complacent before their enemies. "If you wish to know the source from which the Israeli Army draws its strength," said Army Chief of Staff Mordechai Gur during *Yom Ha'Shoah* ceremonies in 1976, "go to the holy martyrs of the Holocaust and the heroes of the revolt. . . . The Holocaust . . . is the root and legitimization of our enterprise."

Yad Vashem

At the center of Israeli Holocaust memory is Yad Vashem, the Holocaust Martyrs' and Heroes' Remembrance Authority in Jerusalem. Established in 1953 by the Knesset, it is Israel's preeminent Holocaust memorial site, museum, and research center.

The Holocaust

At the US Holocaust Memorial Museum in Washington, DC, a wall is filled with photographs of Jewish victims from the town of Eishishok, Lithuania. © Brendan Smialowski/Getty Images.

It was conceived during the war on the assumption that such a memorial could only be in Palestine. But its charter was daunting. On one hand, Yad Vashem was to commemorate all Jews who perished. On the other, it was to honor "the mighty courage of a few, desperate, empty-handed men who went to face the enemy...."

From the start, Yad Vashem struggled to reconcile this dual mission. Initial plans for a Holocaust Hall (to commemorate the murdered) and a Shrine of Heroism (to commemorate fallen Jewish fighters) foundered on objections from Jewish groups abroad who helped finance the site. Moshe Carmel, who moved to Palestine in 1924 and led a brigade in Israel's War of Independence [in 1948], argued that pity for those who simply hoped to survive must have limits. Where would Israel be with such attitudes? Scholar and survivor Nachman Blumenthal differed. "Death," he said, "should not be a matter of discrimination." The passage of time—and particularly the Eichmann trial [in 1961, Adolf Eichmann was the chief administrator of the Holocaust]—increased understanding that Jews were not so neatly divided between a few armed resistors and a mass of passive victims.

Yad Vashem's memorial landscape thus includes the solemn Hall of Remembrance (1961) with the names of Nazi murder sites, ashes of the dead, and an eternal flame; a memorial to Janusz Korczak and the orphans of Warsaw (1978); the Children's Monument, for the 1.5 million children who perished in the Holocaust (1988); and the Valley of the Communities (1992), in which 5,000 names of lost Jewish communities are carved in stone. Yet it also includes the heroic broadly defined—a reproduction of Rapoport's Warsaw Ghetto Monument (1976); the Memorial to Jewish Soldiers, in which a giant sword reaches for the heavens through six massive blocks resembling tombstones (1985); and the Pillar of Heroism (1974), a twenty-one-meter column towering over the entire site, which commemorates all Jewish heroes, from ghetto fighters to all who risked and gave their lives for others.

During the early arguments over Yad Vashem in 1954, a different kind of memorial was begun in the Judean Hills near Jerusalem—the Holocaust Martyrs' Forest. For early Zionist settlers, the planting of trees connected Jews to the homeland both physically and spiritually. It symbolized return to the land, described in the Hebrew Bible as green and abundant. Yet the planting of trees is also a way to redeem the dead. The Holocaust Martyrs' Forest will soon have 6 million trees. With 7,500 acres, it is the largest of all commemorative spaces. It also claims the memory of the 6 million lost as Israel's own. "The memory of our six million holy ones," read the official announcement, "will be eternalized in the trees which will be planted in the earth closest to the heart of each and every Jew."

America's Holocaust Museum

A broad Holocaust consciousness emerged in the United States in the late 1960s and 1970s. The Six Day War of 1967 and the Yom Kippur War of 1972 reminded American Jews of Israel's

Warsaw Ghetto Uprising

The Warsaw Ghetto Uprising was the largest instance of Jewish resistance to the Holocaust. Preparations for it began in late 1942 when some of the Jews in the ghetto, Poland's largest, decided that dying while fighting was a better choice than going to their deaths quietly as most Jews—who still refusing or unable to believe what was truly in store—were doing.

Nazi officials began to liquidate the Warsaw Ghetto in July 1942, steadily shipping groups of victims away, mostly to the Treblinka death camp. Future ghetto fighters, many of them young and already Zionist activists, planned for armed resistance to such measures. Eventually two separate fighting groups emerged, the Jewish Combat Organization and the Jewish Military Union, although numbers of actual fighters were relatively small due to the lack of weapons and munitions.

The first incident of armed resistance took place on January 18, 1943, when, after a hiatus of several months, Nazi forces returned to resume deportations. In a series of small skirmishes, the Jewish fighters managed to force Nazi troops from the ghetto. Over the following weeks, the fighting groups took effective control of the ghetto while most of the remaining Jews, some 50,000 of them, prepared hiding places.

---

vulnerability. A 1978 neo-Nazi march in Skokie, Illinois—the home to many Holocaust survivors—raised the specter of anti-semitism. The realization in the 1970s that several thousand low-level Nazi collaborators immigrated to the United States after the war posing as legitimate refugees was an affront to what the United States represented. A highly successful 1978 television miniseries entitled *Holocaust* brought the murder of Europe's Jews into American living rooms.

Perhaps as an act of reconciliation for his difficult relationship with Israel and American Jewish groups, President Jimmy Carter

Nazi forces returned to the ghetto on April 19, 1943, the eve of the Jewish Passover holiday. They planned to complete their deportations but instead faced determined Jewish fighters armed with Molotov cocktails, improvised explosives, and what few firearms they could locate. This main portion of the Warsaw Ghetto Uprising lasted into May. At one point, Jewish fighters raised both the Polish flag and the blue and white Jewish fighter's flag over the ghetto, symbolizing the claim that the ghetto might now be considered Jewish sovereign territory.

Nazi missteps resulted in the arrival of SS General Juergen Stroop to lead the fight in the ghetto. He proceeded with tactics designed to empty Jewish hiding places block by block using smoke, tear gas, and explosives. As people were marched away to be deported, the Jewish fighters continued their efforts but their numbers and weapons steadily dwindled. Many fighters escaped through Warsaw's sewer system, but others, including leader Mordechai Anielowicz, chose to commit suicide instead. On May 16, Stroop ordered the destruction of Warsaw's largest Jewish temple, the Tlomatskie Synagogue. Although small incidents continued for months, the synagogue's destruction marked the end of the Warsaw Ghetto Uprising.

Many of the surviving ghetto fighters immigrated to Israel after World War II, with many of them living in a special ghetto fighters' kibbutz (an Israeli communal farm or village). Israel's Holocaust Remembrance Day, first celebrated in 1953, coincides with the April 19 anniversary of the uprising.

in 1978 created a Presidential Commission on the Holocaust. It was made up of Jewish survivors, scholars, and advocates as well as non-Jewish elected officials. Its charge was to recommend "an appropriate memorial to those who perished in the Holocaust." The next year, the commission proposed a "living memorial . . . that can transform the living by transmitting the legacy of the Holocaust." The result was the United States Holocaust Memorial Museum, built adjacent to the national mall in Washington, DC, and completed in 1993. It serves as a memorial, museum, research center, and educational resource.

The museum's conceptual process triggered impassioned debate among Jews and gentiles in the United States and elsewhere. One issue was the definition of the Holocaust in an increasingly pluralistic American society. Was it defined by Hitler's singular war against the Jews? Or should it be understood to encompass all of Hitler's victims, thus risking a dilution of its uniqueness and its Jewish core? How to memorialize a foreign catastrophe in a landscape that included soaring memorials to Washington, Jefferson, and Lincoln? And how to represent the terrible events? Should displays, like the Holocaust itself, contain no satisfying ending? Or should they draw out a far-reaching message based on the American insistence on broader lessons and redemption?

These debates brought some scholars, including Israel's Yehuda Bauer, to worry about an "Americanization of the Holocaust." But American Jewish scholar Michael Berenbaum, who helped to shape the museum in a number of leadership roles, understood the careful balance. For American Jews, he wrote, the Holocaust acted less to discredit the Diaspora than it did to "reinforce their commitment to pluralism by recalling the atrocities that sprang from intolerance." And while maintaining its Jewish center, Berenbaum continued, the Holocaust had to be explained to all Americans in a way that would resonate with them. If successful, such an explanation could "provide insights that have universal import for the destiny of all humanity."

Indeed America's Holocaust museum succeeds. With its austere structure that recalls ghettos and camps yet still allows sunlight, with its Jewish yet inclusive themes that embrace diverse individual testimonies, with its deeply personal exhibitions that include family photographs and tactile artifacts painstakingly collected from all over Europe, and with its contemplative yet secular spaces, the museum attracted 30 million visitors as of March 2010. It leaves a mark on all who visit. It also provides a warning, not against Jewish weakness, but against ignorance and, above all, against indifference to the fate of one's fellow human beings, whoever they may be, wherever they may live.

Chapter 2

Controversies and Perspectives

Chapter Exercises

JEWISH EMIGRATION FROM GERMANY, 1933–1939

Destination	Number*
United States	63,000
Palestine	55,000
Great Britain	40,000
France	30,000
Argentina	25,000
Brazil	13,000
South Africa	5,500
Italy	5,000
Other European countries	25,000
Other South American countries	15,000
Other	8,000
Total	**284,500**

* Includes Jews who emigrated from areas occupied by Germany in May 1939.

Source: Judah Gribetz with Edward L. Greenstein and Regina S. Stein, *The Timetables of Jewish History: A Chronology of the Most Important People and Events in Jewish History.* New York: Simon and Schuster, 1993, p. 400.

1. Analyze the Table

Question 1: Which two European nations welcomed the most German Jewish immigrants?

Question 2: Would Jews who went to France be safe from the Holocaust?

Question 3: How many German Jewish refugees went to destinations in North and South America?

2. Writing Prompt

As if you were on the editorial staff of a newspaper, or the author of a well-respected blog, write an editorial arguing that although US officials saw the defeat of Nazi Germany as their main goal during World War II, they might have done more to help European Jews both before and during the Holocaust.

3. Group Activity

Form groups and debate whether Nazi dictator Adolf Hitler always planned to try to massacre Europe's Jews or whether, instead, such policies developed because of the circumstances of World War II in Eastern Europe.

Viewpoint 1

Adolf Hitler Always Planned to Rid Europe of Jews

Kevin P. Sweeney

Experts and scholars still debate whether the Holocaust was the result of Nazi dictator Adolf Hitler's planning or whether it resulted, instead, from wartime circumstances and the decisions of bureaucrats. In the following viewpoint, scholar Kevin P. Sweeney argues that, from an early point in his political career, Hitler always considered the massacre of Europe's Jews a real possibility. He suggests that the lack of a written Holocaust order on Hitler's part is understandable, since any such record was likely destroyed. Meanwhile, other statements found in speeches, diaries, and memoirs make it clear enough, Sweeney claims, that the Holocaust was the product of Hitler's desires and commands. Kevin P. Sweeney has taught at Illinois Wesleyan University.

The "Intentionalist vs. Functionalist" debate has raged amongst academic historians for decades, centered on the question of whether Adolf Hitler personally premeditated and instigated the Final Solution, or whether the idea and its implementation developed out of a collaborative effort within the

Kevin P. Sweeney, "We Will Never Speak of It: Evidence of Hitler's Direct Responsibility for the Premeditation and Implementation of the Nazi Final Solution," *Constructing the Past*, vol. 13, no. 1, Digital Commons/Illinois Wesleyan University, 2012. Copyright © 2012 by Kevin Sweeney. All rights reserved. Reproduced by permission.

ranks of the Nazi bureaucracy. This debate has largely been fueled by the fact that no written decree from Hitler directly ordering the Final Solution has ever been found. However, evidence in the form of personal statements made by Hitler as well as verbal recollections, diary entries, and wartime documents made by his Nazi colleagues point to the idea that he did indeed personally order the Final Solution. Overall, through careful examination of Nazi primary source materials, Hitler's direct responsibility for the premeditation and implementation of the systematic annihilation of European Jewry can be firmly established.

Critics of the idea that Hitler personally developed and instigated the Final Solution generally point to the absence of a Führer-signed decree ordering this genocidal campaign as evidence for their position. However, there is good reason why, in spite of Hitler's being directly responsible for implementing the Final Solution, a written order has never been found: his desire to avoid public association with it for fear of outrage and reprisal, both domestic and international, over his brutal policies of mass murder. An example of the public outrage Hitler feared is seen in the negative reaction of the German populace to his official authorization of the T4 euthanasia program. In general Hitler had a fixed policy of not issuing written instructions for policies relating to what would later be classified as crimes against humanity. However, he made an exception in the case of the T4 euthanasia program, in order to overcome opposition to it within the German state bureaucracy. In a 1939 written decree, Hitler charged program head Reichsleiter Philip Bouhler, and lead program physician Dr. Karl Brandt, with "the responsibility for expanding the authority of physicians . . . to the end that patients considered incurable . . . can be granted mercy death." However, Hitler quickly came to regret authorizing the program in writing, as throughout 1940 the general population became increasingly aware that thousands of mentally and physically disabled Germans were being 'mercy-killed' by the Nazis in a Hitler-sanctioned state program. Between 1940 and 1941 the German people's negative reaction became increasingly vocal and vehement, culminating in Hitler being openly jeered by a crowd watching mentally challenged patients being loaded onto a train at a rail station in Hof, Bavaria in 1941. Ultimately, this negative public reaction to the T4 program and Hitler's sanctioning of it, bolstered by denunciations from Catholic and Protestant church leaders, forced Hitler to publicly cancel the program in August of 1941, though it continued in secret until 1945. Overall, no direct Hitler order for the Final Solution has ever been found due to the public relations debacle that erupted over his sanctioning of the T4 program, as well as its successful continuation in secret following its public 'cancellation'. These events reinforced for Hitler the value of carrying out his programs of systematic murder covertly without written orders, and subsequently informed his methodology for implementing the Final Solution.

Many Documents Were Lost

Even if we ignore the aforementioned evidence for why Hitler never issued a written Final Solution order and hypothetically suppose that one did at some point exist, its absence from the historical record can still be explained as being due to the large-scale destruction of documents and other physical evidence of the Holocaust by the Nazis in the waning days of the war. As their impending defeat became increasingly clear in 1944 and into 1945, the Nazi regime began a desperate undertaking to destroy all documentary evidence of their various crimes against humanity, including internal reports, personal correspondence, and various propaganda materials. In addition, crematoria were knocked down, bodies were exhumed from mass graves and burned, and certain concentration camps were even partially or entirely razed. Following the basic Nazi logic of hoping to evade Allied prosecution for their crimes by covering their tracks, if a piece of evidence as damning as a written decree from Hitler ordering the Final Solution ever did exist, it surely would have been one of the first documents destroyed in this effort. Overall,

T-4 Program

Wartime, Adolf Hitler suggested, "was the best time for the elimination of the incurably ill." Many Germans did not want to be reminded of individuals who did not measure up to their concept of a "master race." The physically and mentally handicapped were viewed as "useless" to society, a threat to Aryan genetic purity, and, ultimately, unworthy of life. At the beginning of World War II, individuals who were mentally retarded, physically handicapped, or mentally ill were targeted for murder in what the Nazis called the "T-4," or "euthanasia," program.

The "euthanasia" program required the cooperation of many German doctors, who reviewed the medical files of patients in institutions to determine which handicapped or mentally ill individuals should be killed. The doctors also supervised the actual killings. Doomed patients were transferred to six institutions in Germany and Austria, where they were killed in specially constructed gas chambers. Handicapped infants and small children were also killed by injection with a deadly dose of drugs or by starvation. The bodies of the victims were burned in large ovens called *crematoria*.

Despite public protests in 1941, the Nazi leadership continued this program in secret throughout the war. About 200,000 handicapped people were murdered between 1940 and 1945.

The T-4 program became the model for the mass murder of Jews, Roma (Gypsies), and others in camps equipped with gas chambers that the Nazis would open in 1941 and 1942. The program also served as a training ground for SS members who manned these camps.

"The Murder of the Handicapped," United States Holocaust Memorial Museum. www.ushmm.org.

even if Hitler had issued a written order directly sanctioning the Final Solution, it surely would not have survived the Nazis' desperate late-war attempts to destroy the evidence of their crimes against humanity.

Early Statements

Since no definitive written order is known to exist, modern scholars must turn to alternative sources of primary evidence in determining Hitler's direct responsibility for developing and implementing the Final Solution. One of the most important of these sources is the abundance of transcripts of Hitler's public statements and speeches regarding the 'Jewish Question'. The earliest piece of verbal evidence from Hitler pointing to his personal premeditation of the Final Solution is a statement he made to journalist Josef Hell during an interview in 1922:

> Once I really am in power, my first and foremost task will be the annihilation of the Jews. As soon as I have the power to do so, I will have gallows built in rows. . . . Then the Jews will be hanged indiscriminately . . . until all of Germany has been completely cleansed of Jews.

This statement clearly shows that even long prior to taking power, Hitler had begun premeditating, at least in its most basic form, a campaign of genocide against Germany's Jews, and that he personally desired the systematic destruction of the Jewish race. Another statement by Hitler that points to his personal premeditation of the Final Solution is one he made to Czech foreign minister František Chvalkovský during a meeting on January 21, 1939: "We are going to destroy the Jews. They are not going to get away with what they did on 9 November 1918. The day of reckoning has come." Hitler reiterated this genocidal sentiment nine days later in his "prophecy" speech before the Reichstag: "If International Jewry . . . should succeed once more in plunging nations into another world war, the consequence will be . . . the annihilation of the Jewish race in Europe." Hitler further emphasized his 'prophecy' regarding the fate of eradication for Europe's Jews during a speech in Munich to commemorate the 19th anniversary of his failed 'Beer Hall Putsch', on November 8, 1942:

You will recall the Reichstag session during which I declared: "if Jewry should bring about a world war, the result will be . . . the extermination of Jewry in Europe." People laughed about me as a prophet. Of those who laughed then, countless numbers no longer laugh today, and those who still laugh now will no longer laugh a short time from now.

Overall, these recorded statements publicly made by Hitler prior to and during his twelve-year reign over Germany clearly show his personal calculation of and desire for the Final Solution.

Claiming Hitler's Authority

In addition to the personal statements and speeches that convey Hitler's premeditation of the Final Solution, private records and wartime documents generated by high-ranking Nazi bureaucrats point to his personal ordering of it. An example of this can be seen in a diary entry by Minister of Propaganda Joseph Goebbels dated to December 12, 1941: "With respect of the Jewish Question, the Führer has decided to make a clean sweep. He prophesied to the Jews that if they again brought about a world war, they would live to see their annihilation in it. That wasn't just a catch-word. The world war is here and the annihilation of the Jews must be the necessary consequence." A year later, on February 14, 1942, Goebbels again made reference in his diary to Hitler's ordering of the Final Solution: "The Führer once again expressed his determination to clean up the Jews in Europe pitilessly . . . Their destruction will go hand in hand with the destruction of our enemies . . . The Führer expressed this idea vigorously and repeated it afterward to a group of officers." An additional reference to Hitler personally being the point of origin of the Final Solution is seen in a diary entry by Goebbels dated to March 2, 1943, in which he states: "As always in the circles of the party, it is the duty of the Führer's closest friends to gather around him in times of need . . . Above all with regard to the Jewish question . . . we are so fixed on it that there is no longer any escape." Another private Nazi record that points to Hitler's

The Holocaust

Nazi leader Adolf Hitler salutes members of the German Luftwaffe at a 1939 rally. © Hugo Jaeger/Timepix/Time Life Pictures/Getty Images.

having ordered the Final Solution is a handwritten note by Reichsführer-SS Heinrich Himmler from a meeting with Hitler at the Wolfsschanze ["Wolf's Lair," a military headquarters] on December 18, 1941, which simply read: "Jewish Question / to be exterminated like the partisans." A final example of an internal Reich record that points to Hitler being directly responsible for the move to exterminate the Jewish race is the transcript of his meeting with Palestinian leader Mufti Haj Amin al-Husseini, on 28 November 1941, as recorded by Dr. Paul Otto Schmidt. From Schmidt's meeting minutes, we clearly see that Hitler directly promised al-Husseini that "He (the Führer) would carry on the fight until the last traces of the Jewish-Communist European hegemony had been obliterated." The meeting notes also show that Hitler subsequently promised Husseini that once the Nazis gained control of the Southern Caucasus, "Germany's only remaining objective in the region would be limited to the annihilation of the Jews living under British protection in Arab lands." Overall, these internal Nazi documents clearly show that Hitler not only sanctioned the Final Solution, but actively planned and gave the orders to instigate it.

Postwar Recollections

In addition to the aforementioned Nazi writings and internal documents, a number of recollections of conversations and verbal admissions made by high ranking Nazi bureaucrats also point directly to Hitler having personally ordered the Final Solution. An example of this is seen in an excerpt from Auschwitz Commandant Rudolf Hoess' memoirs, detailing a meeting he had with Heinrich Himmler in the summer of 1941: "Himmler received me and said in effect: 'The Führer has ordered that the Jewish question be solved once and for all and that we, the SS, are to implement that order . . . The Jews are the sworn enemies of the German people and must be eradicated.'" In addition to this, former SS-Obersturmbannführer Adolf Eichmann, during a 1960 interrogation in Israel by police officer Avner Less, was recorded as saying

> The war with the Soviet Union began in June 1941. I believe it was two months later that [SS-Obergruppenführer Reinhard] Heydrich sent for me. I reported . . . He began with a little speech. And then: "The Führer has ordered physical extermination of the Jews.". . . Then Heydrich said: "Go and see [SS-Obergruppenführer Odilo] Globocnik, the Führer has already given him instructions."

Another verbal Nazi admission that the order for the Final Solution was generated by Hitler comes from the 1947 trial of Einsatzgruppen commander, SS-Obersturmbannführer Dr. Martin Sandberger, during which he stated: "I myself was present during the discussions in the Palais Prinz Albrecht in Berlin and during the speech by [SS-Gruppenführer Bruno] Streckenbach when the well-known Führer order was announced . . .

Streckenbach personally informed me about the Führer order, which said that, in order to secure the Eastern territory permanently all Jews ... were to be eliminated." A final recollection that verbally points to Hitler's personally ordering the Final Solution comes from an excerpt of the memoirs of Heinrich Himmler's personal masseur, Felix Kersten, in which he recounts a conversation with his boss:

> I said that the world would no longer tolerate the extermination of the Jews; it was high time that he put a stop to it. Himmler said that it was beyond his power; he was not the Führer and Adolf Hitler had expressly ordered it . . . I told him he should think of his reputation, not sully it with that reproach. Himmler replied that he had done nothing wrong and only carried out Adolf Hitler's orders.

Overall, these various recollections by Nazi bureaucrats and Reich insiders point to Hitler's directly ordering and leading the implementation of the Final Solution.

Viewpoint 2

The Holocaust Began Because of Circumstances Rather than a Longstanding Plan

Gordon McFee

In the following viewpoint, essayist Gordon McFee argues that the Holocaust resulted from a collection of actions and decisions made by Nazi troops and officials in the second half of 1941. Adolf Hitler, he suggests, did indeed order the massacre of European Jews; in a dictatorial system, such a decision could only come from the supreme leader. But Hitler only issued his order after the killings had already begun, and after battlefield setbacks and the entrance of the United States into World War II promised a much longer, harder war than he had originally envisioned. By contrast, no hard evidence exists to suggest that Hitler consciously planned for mass murder before the end of 1941. Gordon McFee is a senior civil servant with the government of Canada and a graduate of universities in both Canada and Germany. He is the author of a number of essays on the Holocaust.

One of the most interesting, and hotly debated, aspects of the Holocaust is when Hitler ordered it to begin.

The thinking to now has been that the decision was made in early to mid 1941, and that it got into full gear in early 1942.

Gordon McFee, "When Did Hitler Decide on the Final Solution?," The Holocaust History Project, July 13, 2011. www.holocaust-history.org. Copyright © 2001 by Gordon McFee. All rights reserved. Reproduced by permission.

The Holocaust

That thinking is now challenged by the recent discovery of hitherto unavailable documents, recently uncovered by German historian Christian Gerlach. The new documents include a diary entry by Propaganda Minister Joseph Goebbels of December 12, 1941 and a portion of Reichsführer-SS Heinrich Himmler's diary entry of December 18, 1941.

Current Thinking

Before getting to these recent discoveries and what they mean, it is in order to briefly recapitulate the current state of thinking on the matter. It is generally accepted that the decision was made to physically exterminate the Jews in early to mid 1941. Hitler's secretary remembers a private meeting between Himmler and Hitler in the early spring of 1941, after which Himmler sat at [his] desk with a very troubled look on his face, put his head in his hands and said: "My God, my God, what I am expected to do." She is convinced that that was the day Hitler ordered him to murder the Jews. Other accounts suppose that the decision was made roughly around the time between March 1941 and the invasion of the Soviet Union. (Research in this area is hampered by the fact that no written Hitler-Order launching the Final Solution has ever been found, and that if there ever was one, it most likely was destroyed.) Rudolf Hoess, commandant of Auschwitz and Adolf Eichmann, head of Amt [Office] IVB4 (Jewish Affairs) both speak of having been told of a Hitler-Order in early summer of 1941.

Historians have generally thought that the Final Solution unfolded like this. First, the Einsatzgruppen (special task forces) entered the Soviet Union behind the invading armed forces in late June 1941 and began shooting Jews where they were found. Roughly 500,000 Jews were killed in this way between July and December 1941. At that time, the sheer number of Jews to be killed and the effect on the police of shooting women and children caused other methods to be investigated, culminating in the establishment of death camps such as Auschwitz, Treblinka and Sobibor in early 1942, to which Jews were transported and gassed with carbon monoxide or prussic acid (Zyklon B).

This raises several questions, such as:

- If the decision had already been made in early 1941 (before the invasion of the Soviet Union), what was the point of Goering issuing his Final Solution order to Reinhard Heydrich (Chief of the Reich Security Main Office and in charge of the Final Solution along with Himmler) of July 31, 1941?
- Why did Heydrich wait until January 1942 to hold the Wannsee Conference, where the administrative planning for the Final Solution was finalized?
- Where is the Hitler-Order that set all this in place?

The recent discoveries allude to a clear and unambiguous order from Hitler himself to kill the Jews. At the same time, they suggest three revisions to the current theory may be in order. First, it is now *undeniable* that Hitler personally ordered the overall Final Solution decision; second, the decision was *not* made prior to the invasion of the Soviet Union—rather, the ultimate decision was taken near the end of 1941; third, the Final Solution was not a smoothly evolving process, but rather more dependent on the vagaries of the war effort.

The Recently Discovered Documents

The two recent discoveries are:

1. The first is a diary entry by Joseph Goebbels of December 12, 1941. It runs as follows:

    With respect of the Jewish Question, the Führer has decided to make a clean sweep. He prophesied to the Jews that if they again brought about a world war, they would live to see their annihilation in it. That wasn't just a catchword. The world war is here, and the annihilation of the Jews must be the necessary consequence.

2. The second is a note in his own handwriting by Reichsführer-SS Heinrich Himmler in his soon to be published diary of a meeting he had with Hitler at the latter's Headquarters on December 18, 1941. The notes are simply:

> Jewish Question / to be exterminated like the partisans.

Hitler Personally Ordered the Final Solution

Most experts have agreed that an action on the magnitude of a mass genocide, with the resultant possible ramifications, could not have proceeded without Hitler's personal approval. Until now, no written decision from Hitler has been found, although there are compelling indications that a verbal decision was certainly given. The recent discoveries cannot be called a written decision (which, if it ever existed, was almost certainly destroyed by the end of the war), but they are certainly unequivocal confirmation that a clear decision was taken by Hitler. Even better, they help pinpoint the time it was taken.

The Decision Was Made at the End of 1941

The new evidence strongly suggests that Hitler decided once and for all, in early December 1941, to exterminate all of European Jewry. That squares with the words, "aspired final solution" in Goering's order to Heydrich of July 1941, and helps to explain why the Wannsee Conference took place so long after the Goering order had been issued, that is, the final order had still not been given in July 1941.

This does not mean that no order at all had been given at the time of the invasion of the Soviet Union. Indeed, it is certain that an order to kill Jews, commissars and other "undesirables" had been given before the Soviet invasion, and it may well be that order that Hitler's secretary refers to. It most likely took the form of Hitler telling Himmler that as part of the invasion, the individuals mentioned above would be systematically killed and

Jewish men and women stand near the barbed wire fence of the ghetto in Kutno, Poland, in early 1940. © Hugo Jaeger/Timepix/Time Life Pictures/Getty Images.

that Himmler was charged with execution of the order. And it is most likely this order that Eichmann, Hoess and others referred to in their various testimonies.

But in addition to that, these individuals would have been aware of Goering's order for the administrative work to be done towards an "aspired" final solution. Everyone knew that a *final solution*—a decision to annihilate all of European Jewry—could only be made by Hitler. And Hitler was legendary for hesitating, at times with almost disastrous effects, when faced with grave decisions. . . . It would be entirely in keeping with Hitler's personality if he hesitated several months after ordering the Einsatzgruppen shootings—a kind of pre-final solution—before he could bring himself to make the ultimate decision. Goering's order notwithstanding, there was little concrete action that Heydrich could take until there was a definitive decision from the man at the top. And the man at the top did not decide until December 1941.

One can only speculate what finally catalysed Hitler into making the ultimate decision in December 1941, but a look at the situation at that time suggests several factors played a role. First, with the Japanese attack on Pearl Harbor, the American declaration of war to Japan, and Hitler's own declaration of war against the United States, Hitler now had the "world" war referred to by Goebbels in his diary entry of December 12, 1941. Second, the first great reversal of German fortunes in the war against the Soviet Union had taken place. On December 5, at the very gates of Moscow, the German army was stopped [in] its tracks by the onset of a vicious Russian winter. Temperatures dropped to 31 degrees below zero that day, and the next day to 36 below. The Germans were not equipped with winter gear, the panzers broke down, and, on the 6th, [Russian] General Georgi Zhukov attacked on [the] 200-mile front before Moscow with 100 divisions that the Germans had not even known existed. Hitler must have known at this stage that his war effort was in serious, perhaps grave danger. Third, the sheer numbers of Jews to be killed and the difficulties doing it caused for the police who did the shooting were passed on by Himmler to Hitler. There had been discussions on the use of poisonous gas as a means of killing Jews and avoiding public spectacles that sometimes accompanied shooting throughout the autumn of 1941.

Against this backdrop, it can be plausibly argued that December 1941 was a kind of watershed for Hitler. The congruence of events may well have forced him into a position where he burned his bridges.

VIEWPOINT 3

Only the Pressures of War Turned Ordinary Germans into Killers

Christopher R. Browning

Historian Christopher R. Browning argues in the following viewpoint that most members of a group of Nazi murderers he studied, Reserve Order Police Battalion 101, became killers because of the circumstances of war and occupation. He puts forward that, like other soldiers in other contexts, including American ones, ordinary German men were "brutalized" by their wartime experiences and eventually grew accustomed to atrocities. Reserve Order Police Battalion 101 was stationed in occupied Poland to provide increased behind-the-lines security rather than serve as frontline soldiers; however, members found themselves ordered to take part in a number of anti-Jewish "actions" as well, including, sometimes, the close-range shootings of villagers. Browning estimates they were connected to the killings of tens of thousands of Polish Jews. Christopher R. Browning is the Frank Porter Graham Professor of History at the University of North Carolina and a fellow of the American Academy of Arts and Sciences. His books include Remembering Survival: Inside a Nazi Slave Labor Camp, The Origins of the Final Solution: The Evolution of Nazi Jewish Policy, September 1939–March 1942 *and* The Final Solution and the German Foreign Office.

Excerpted from *Ordinary Men: Reserve Police Battalion 101 and the Final Solution in Poland* by Christopher R. Browning, pp. 159–65. Copyright © 1992, 1998 by Christopher Browning. Reprinted by permission of HarperCollins Publishers.

The Holocaust

Why did most men in Reserve Police Battalion 101 become killers, while only a minority of perhaps 10 percent—and certainly no more than 20 percent—did not? A number of explanations have been invoked in the past to explain such behavior: wartime brutalization, racism, segmentation and routinization of the task, special selection of the perpetrators, careerism, obedience to orders, deference to authority, ideological indoctrination, and conformity. These factors are applicable in varying degrees, but none without qualification.

Wars have invariably been accompanied by atrocities. As [historian] John Dower has noted in his remarkable book, *War Without Mercy: Race and Power in the Pacific War*, "war hates" induce "war crimes." Above all, when deeply embedded negative racial stereotypes are added to the brutalization inherent in sending armed men to kill one another on a massive scale, the fragile tissue of war conventions and rules of combat is even more frequently and viciously broken on all sides. Hence the difference between more conventional war—between Germany and the Western allies, for example—and the "race wars" of the recent past. From the Nazi "war of destruction" in eastern Europe and "war against the Jews" to the "war without mercy" in the Pacific and most recently Vietnam, soldiers have all too often tortured and slaughtered unarmed civilians and helpless prisoners, and committed numerous other atrocities. Dower's account of entire American units in the Pacific openly boasting of a "take no prisoners" policy and routinely collecting body parts of Japanese soldiers as battlefield souvenirs is chilling reading for anyone who smugly assumes that war atrocities were a monopoly of the Nazi regime.

Battlefield Frenzy

War, and especially race war, leads to brutalization, which leads to atrocity. This common thread, it could be argued, runs from Bromberg and Babi Yar [earlier Nazi massacres] through New Guinea and Manila [in World War II] and on to My Lai [in the Vietnam War]. But if war, and especially race war, was a vital context within which Reserve Police Battalion 101 operated (as I shall indeed argue), how much does the notion of wartime brutalization explain the specific behavior of the policemen at Józefów and after? In particular, what distinctions must be made between various kinds of war crimes and the mind-sets of the men who commit them?

Many of the most notorious wartime atrocities—Oradour and Malmédy, the Japanese rampage through Manila, the American slaughter of prisoners and mutilation of corpses on many Pacific islands [all in World War II], and the massacre at My Lai—involved a kind of "battlefield frenzy." Soldiers who were inured to violence, numbed to the taking of human life, embittered over their own casualties, and frustrated by the tenacity of an insidious and seemingly inhuman enemy sometimes exploded and at other times grimly resolved to have their revenge at the first opportunity. Though atrocities of this kind were too often tolerated, condoned, or tacitly (sometimes even explicitly) encouraged by elements of the command structure, they did not represent official government policy. Despite the hate-filled propaganda of each nation and the exterminatory rhetoric of many leaders and commanders, such atrocities still represented a breakdown in discipline and the chain of command. They were not "standard operating procedure."

Other kinds of atrocity, lacking the immediacy of battlefield frenzy and fully expressing official government policy, decidedly were "standard operating procedure." The fire-bombing of German and Japanese cities, the enslavement and murderous maltreatment of foreign laborers in German camps and factories or along the Siam-Burma railroad, the reprisal shooting of a hundred civilians for every German soldier killed by partisan attack in Yugoslavia or elsewhere in eastern Europe [all in World War II]—these were not the spontaneous explosions or cruel revenge of brutalized men but the methodically executed policies of government.

Both kinds of atrocities occur in the brutalizing context of war, but the men who carry out "atrocity by policy" are in a different state of mind. They act not out of frenzy, bitterness, and frustration but with calculation. Clearly the men of Reserve Police Battalion 101, in implementing the systematic Nazi policy of exterminating European Jewry, belong in the second category. Except for a few of the oldest men who were veterans of World War I, and a few NCOs [noncommissioned officers] who had been transferred to Poland from Russia, the men of the battalion had not seen battle or encountered a deadly enemy. Most of them had not fired a shot in anger or ever been fired on, much less lost comrades fighting at their side. Thus, wartime brutalization through prior combat was not an immediate experience directly influencing the policemen's behavior at Józefów [the site of Battalion 101's first massacre in Poland]. Once the killing began, however, the men became increasingly brutalized. As in combat, the horrors of the initial encounter eventually became routine, and the killing became progressively easier. In this sense, brutalization was not the cause but the effect of these men's behavior.

The context of war must surely be taken into account in a more general way than as a cause of combat-induced brutalization and frenzy, however. War, a struggle between "our people" and "the enemy," creates a polarized world in which "the enemy" is easily objectified and removed from the community of human obligation. War is the most conducive environment in which governments can adopt "atrocity by policy" and encounter few difficulties in implementing it. As John Dower has observed, "The Dehumanization of the Other contributed immeasurably to the psychological distancing that facilitated killing." Distancing, not frenzy and brutalization, is one of the keys to the behavior of Reserve Police Battalion 101. War and negative racial stereotyping were two mutually reinforcing factors in this distancing....

Not Dedicated Killers

To what degree, if any, did the men of Reserve Police Battalion 101 represent a process of special selection for the particular task of implementing the Final Solution? According to recent research by the German historian Hans-Heinrich Wilhelm, considerable time and effort was expended by the personnel department of [SS deputy chief] Reinhard Heydrich's Reich Security Main Office to select and assign officers for the Einsatzgruppen [special shooting squads]. [SS chief Heinrich] Himmler, anxious to get the right man for the right job, was also careful in his selection of Higher SS and Police Leaders and others in key positions. Hence his insistence on keeping the unsavory [SS officer Odilo] Globocnik in Lublin, despite his past record of corruption and objections to his appointment even within the Nazi Party. In her book *Into That Darkness,* a classic study of Franz Stangl, the commandant of Treblinka [a death camp], Gitta Sereny concluded that special care must have been taken to choose just 96 of some 400 people to be transferred from the euthanasia program [the Nazis' killing of the mentally and physically disabled] in Germany to the death camps in Poland. Did any similar policy of selection, the careful choosing of personnel particularly suited for mass murder, determine the makeup of Reserve Police Battalion 101?

Concerning the rank and file, the answer is a qualified no. By most criteria, in fact, just the opposite was the case. By age, geographical origin, and social background, the men of Reserve Police Battalion 101 were least likely to be considered apt material out of which to mold future mass killers. On the basis of these criteria, the rank and file—middle-aged, mostly working-class, from Hamburg—did not represent special selection or even random selection but for all practical purposes negative selection for the task at hand.

In one respect, however, an earlier and more general form of selection may have taken place. The high percentage (25 percent) of Party members among the battalion's rank and file, particularly disproportionate for those of working-class origin, suggests that the initial conscription of reservists—long before their use as killers in the Final Solution was envisaged—was not entirely random. If Himmler at first thought of the reservists as a potential internal security force while large numbers of active police were stationed abroad, it is logical that he would have been leery of conscripting men of dubious political reliability. One solution would have been to draft middle-aged Party members for reserve duty in higher proportions than from the population at large. But the existence of such a policy is merely a suspicion, for no documents have been found to prove that Party members were deliberately drafted into the reserve units of the Order Police.

Not Top Nazis

The case for special selection of officers is even more difficult to make. By SS standards, Major Trapp [commander of Reserve Police Battalion 101] was a patriotic German but traditional and overly sentimental—what in Nazi Germany was scornfully considered both "weak" and "reactionary." It is certainly revealing that despite the conscious effort of Himmler and Heydrich to amalgamate the SS and the police, and despite the fact that Trapp was a decorated World War I veteran, career policeman, and *Alter Kämpfer* [old Nazi fighter] who joined the Party in 1932, he was never taken into the SS. He was certainly not given command of Reserve Police Battalion 101 and specifically assigned to the Lublin district because of his presumed suitability as a mass killer.

The remaining officers of the battalion scarcely evidence a policy of careful selection either. Despite their impeccable Party credentials, both Hoffmann and Wohlauf had been shunted into slow-track careers by SS standards. Wohlauf's career in the Order Police in particular was marked by mediocre, even negative, evaluations. Ironically, it was the relatively old (forty-eight) Reserve Lieutenant Gnade, not the two young SS captains, who turned out to be the most ruthless and sadistic killer, a man who took pleasure in his work. . . .

In short, Reserve Police Battalion 101 was not sent to Lublin to murder Jews because it was composed of men specially selected or deemed particularly suited for the task. On the contrary, the battalion was the "dregs" of the manpower pool available at that stage of the war. It was employed to kill Jews because it was the only kind of unit available for such behind-the-lines duties. Most likely, Globocnik simply assumed as a matter of course that whatever battalion came his way would be up to this murderous task, regardless of its composition.

Viewpoint 4

It Is Important to Keep Alive the Memory of the Holocaust in the Face of Challenges

Sean Lang

Writing the following viewpoint at the time of the sixtieth anniversary of the liberation of the Auschwitz extermination camp, author Sean Lang touches on the issue of the Holocaust as the source of historical lessons. These lessons include the need to tell the true story of the Holocaust in order to challenge Holocaust denial. In addition, a true understanding of the events helps make clear the desire of the nation of Israel to protect itself and to provide comparisons with more recent examples of mass killings. Another lesson is that ordinary people can be capable of the worst possible crimes. Sean Lang is the author of The Second World War: Conflict and Cooperation, *as well as other books on World War II and twentieth-century history.*

In January 2005, world leaders met at Oswiecim in southern Poland to mark the sixtieth anniversary of the liberation by the Red Army of the notorious extermination camp of Auschwitz. The event attracted wide publicity, with a specially-made drama documentary series on the BBC, long articles in the press, in-

Sean Lang, "Remembering the Holocaust," *20th Century Historical Review*, vol. 1, no. 1, September 2005. Reproduced in adapted form by permission of Philip Allan for Hodder Education. Copyright © 2005 by Hodder Education. All rights reserved. Reproduced by permission.

A 2005 photograph of the Auschwitz Concentration Camp Museum in Oswiecim, Poland, shows the camp's guard tower and multiple layers of high-voltage fences. © Scott Barbour/ Getty Images.

terviews with survivors and, perhaps most worryingly, a survey suggesting that large numbers of people in Britain—particularly young people—did not know what Auschwitz was. If true, this would indeed be worrying, though closer investigation suggested that what people did not know was that the camp had originally been an army barracks, which is rather more understandable.

But why do we keep remembering the Holocaust and what does it mean for us today? The facts remain a matter of dispute. We have detailed evidence of every aspect of the operation of the Holocaust, right down to builders' specifications for gas chambers, but still neo-Nazi groups keep claiming that the Holocaust never happened. When the British writer David Irving tried to prove the point in court, it was conclusively shown that he had systematically distorted or manipulated the evidence and he lost his case.

The memory of the Holocaust is of the highest importance to Jewish people, partly out of respect for the dead, but partly out of

The Holocaust

Death Camps

Most of the victims of the Holocaust were killed by gassing in one of six dedicated death camps. These camps were modeled on the concentration camps that Nazi Germany had maintained since 1933 but were modified and expanded to include special killing facilities and ways of disposing bodies. All six of the death camps were located in or quite close to German-occupied Poland rather than Germany itself.

The Chelmno, or Kulmhof, camp was the first to operate. There, Jews were being murdered in so-called gas vans by late 1941. It remained the smallest of the camps.

Belzec, Sobibor, and Treblinka were where most of the millions of remaining Polish Jews, as well as Jews from elsewhere who were sent to the Polish ghettos, were gassed. Having largely accomplished their goal of making Poland "Judenfrei," or free of

a determination never again to fall into the position of helpless victim of a murderous enemy. You can see elements of this thinking in Israel's determination not to give way before Arab suicide bombers. Other countries have had to face up to their role in the Holocaust. It is obviously painful for the Germans, but the French too have had to come to terms with the extent to which they helped in the process, denouncing Jews to the Germans while French gendarmes rounded them up—children as well—and put them on the trains to Auschwitz. There is similarly painful heart-searching in the Channel Islands, where the British authorities cooperated in rounding up Jews for the camps.

Lessons Learned?

However, remembering the Holocaust is not just about looking back. Teachers often say they teach about it to help ensure that such things will never happen again. Sadly, they do. 2005

> Jews, Nazi officials closed all three camps and dismantled their facilities by the end of 1943.
>
> Majdanek first opened near the Polish city of Lublin as a concentration camp and forced labor center. It was expanded to include murder facilities in 1942 but continued its other functions as well. The camp was liberated by approaching Soviet Russian forces in July 1944. It was the first of the death camps to be exposed.
>
> Auschwitz, in southern Poland, was the largest of the death camps. Originally a camp for captured war prisoners, it opened its first gas chambers in March 1942. The camp expanded rapidly, eventually spawning numerous subcamps for slave laborers. It also grew to include extensive killing facilities and factories engaged in war production. Estimates vary, but at least one million people were killed there. Victims included not only Jews but Roma (Gypsies), Poles, and others. Of all the camps, most is known about Auschwitz thanks to numerous survivors, as well as the fact that—despite attempts—Nazi officials were unable to destroy the camp before abandoning it in January 1945.

also marked the tenth anniversary of the massacre by Serbs of thousands of Muslims at Srebrenica, during the civil wars that tore former Yugoslavia apart in the 1990s. This was part of an attempted genocide of the native Muslim population of Bosnia-Herzegovina. At the same time there was an extraordinary outbreak of genocidal murder in Rwanda, where the Hutu massacred nearly a million Tutsis in a matter of months.

Does this mean that we do not learn from history? Perhaps it means that we are looking to it for the wrong lessons. After all, if you cannot already see that mass murder is wrong, learning about the Holocaust is not likely to change your mind. But the story of the Holocaust does show how ordinary, otherwise decent and compassionate, people ended up taking part in genocide. The pattern at work in Europe in the 1930s was also to be found in the 1990s: a strong sense that the victims posed a threat, a sense that the threat was urgent and required drastic action and, above all, the reassurance that someone higher up would take responsibility for the killing. In this sense the Holocaust remains depressingly relevant to the modern world and it is only right and proper that we should continue to remember it.

VIEWPOINT 5

Holocaust Deniers Often Try to Appear Respectable

Nick Ryan

In the following viewpoint, British writer Nick Ryan looks at the contemporary world of Holocaust deniers. Often calling themselves "historical revisionists"—implying that they are merely offering alternative interpretations of historical evidence—these deniers, as Ryan notes, are often connected to extreme right-wing political groups. Ryan's interviewees include both British and German spokespeople, many connected to the Los Angeles–based "revisionist" organization known as the Institute for Historical Review. He also warns of the dangers of these deniers' distortions of history. Nick Ryan's articles have appeared in newspapers and magazines around the world. He is the author of Homeland *as well as a television production consultant.*

In the midst of increasing antisemitic sentiment and attacks against Jews, ardent Holocaust deniers (or 'historical revisionists' as they like to see themselves) are now finding the perfect opportunity to insinuate their views into the wider discourse.

For a long time such fascists and neo-fascists have talked about 'The Jewish Problem'. During my own investigations into

Nick Ryan, "Demagogues in Denial: the Holocaust 'Revisionist' Industry Is Running a Brisk Trade," *New Internationalist*, vol. 372, October 2004. Copyright © 2004 by New Internationalist. All rights reserved. Reproduced by permission.

the murky world of the extreme Right, I witnessed this hatred of the Jews as the ideological glue which binds together many Far Right organizations, as well as linking them to a wider network of other militants. Just look on the internet for shared theories about 'Zionist conspiracies' regarding 9/11. This was one of the many popular themes espoused by rightwing ideologues and Islamic militants at a large meeting in Beirut to which I was invited. It was organized under the auspices of the Los Angeles-based Institute for Historical Review (IHR), a major force in the revisionist scene.

In Britain, I met many times with Nick Griffin, leader of the British National Party (BNP), a Far Right group which now holds 21 local council seats and has electoral aspirations for national and European parliaments. Though he now denies antisemitism has any relevance to the electorate, Griffin wrote a booklet called "Who are the Mindbenders?" in which he obsessed about supposed Jewish control over the British media and government. He fumed about Holocaust 'lies', invoking the popular phraseology of the Far Right—the Holohoax'.

The BNP leader railed: 'I am well aware that the orthodox opinion is that six million Jews were gassed and cremated . . . Orthodox opinion also once held that the earth is flat . . . I have reached the conclusion that the 'extermination' tale is a mixture of Allied wartime propaganda, extremely profitable lie, and latter-day witch hysteria.'

Travelling down Griffin's network of contacts in the US, I encountered John Tiffany, an aficionado of Celtic culture, in his mid-fifties and a self-educated 'historian'. He edits *The Barnes Review* (TBR) magazine, one of the bibles of the Revisionist movement. For many years it has been controlled behind the scenes by Willis Carto, former aide to pro-segregation politician George Wallace and founder of the Far Right Liberty Lobby pressure group.

The Barnes Review also organizes various conferences and it was at one of these that I met Tiffany. I listened to a lecture by the infamous Fred Leuchter, who claimed to have 'proven' there were no gas chambers and met the smartly dressed Germar Rudolph, who was wanted in Germany (having been sentenced in absentia for Holocaust denial, which is a crime there).

The Barnes Review mission statement is typical of these sorts of Revisionist outfits: 'TBR aims to tell you the truth—the whole truth about history—things you need to know to figure out how things got so screwed up—and why. It's a good investment in your family's future. No other history publication in America can truthfully say that.' A nervous, mumbling speaker, Tiffany, wearing a kilt, explained: 'We're oriented towards the white race and the Germanic peoples and the Celtic peoples, primarily. We think that every race should have pride in its heritage.'

Talking with him was a very matter-of-fact, mundane experience. He seemed like nothing other than a slightly eccentric scholar. 'History is being written by the victors, so all we hear about is the evil Germans,' he declared, his voice passionate. 'A large part of our thrust is towards correcting the "evil Germans" image, the "German Hun", where the Establishment not only blames them for World War One but World War Two, claiming they wanted to exterminate the Jewish people and various other peoples.'

This obsession with the War is something that unites many Revisionists who lambast Jews for supposedly degrading German culture. They ridicule Jewish remembrance of the Shoah by describing it as 'Holocaustianity'.

'We Germans don't have any identity at all. We lost it after the War', explained the soft-spoken, American-accented Horst Mahler. I met Mahler at his house in Berlin, the day after a May Day march by over a thousand neo-Nazi skinheads. They'd been shouting 'Frei, Sozial, und Nation-aal!' ('Free, Social and National'), as they marched in stormtrooper fashion, occasionally exchanging blows with anti-fascist protesters.

Mahler was something of an oddity. He'd been a founding member of the leftwing terrorist group, the Red Army Faction

ESTIMATED NUMBER OF DEATHS AT THE SIX MAJOR NAZI DEATH CAMPS

Camp	Estimated Deaths	Occupied Territory
Auschwitz–Birkenau	1,100,000	Province of Upper Silesia
Bełżec	600,000	General Government district
Chełmno	320,000	District of Reichsgau Wartheland
Majdanek	80,000	General Government district
Sobibor	250,000	General Government district
Treblinka	800,000	General Government district

(also known as the Baader-Meinhof Gang). After a 10-year spell in prison for armed robbery, he reverted to his lawyer's practice then decided to join the neo-Nazi *Nationaldemokratische Partei Deutschland* (NPD—National Democratic Party), defending it against a possible government ban.

I listened to Mahler's ruminating while birds sang incongruously from his garden. 'Everyone now believes that the Nazis were the devil and who wants to give their hand to the devil? But this will change soon.' He paused, perhaps for effect. 'That's why the Government wanted to ban NPD.'

A Return to the Nazi Era?

'People say National Socialism was all bad, only concentration camps, killing people, and this is National Socialism. And if you are a National Socialist you are the devil and we can beat you. And this is untrue.'

Like myself, Mahler had been on the guest list for the IHR revisionist conference in Beirut. He had intricate theories on how President Roosevelt had joined the Second World War thanks to a Jewish conspiracy. He then talked about the resistance to his ideas from the 'New World Order, which is dominated by the One World power now and I guess this will change very soon,' he said, ominously. 'This model will be victorious all over the world and it will start here in Germany.'

One woman knows what it is like to be close to such men. She is Irene Zundel, ex-wife of the Holocaust denier Ernst Zundel, a German national who'd spent many years living in Canada. Zundel created and ran the Zundelsite on the web, a haven for Far Right discussion and thinking. He is now in jail in Canada fighting a high-profile extradition case to Germany on charges of inciting hatred.

'The atmosphere was always paranoid and conspiratorial. Ernst was considered a threat to national security and was convinced he was constantly watched, wiretapped and plotted against from within and without. He recorded or listened to all my calls with friends and family, read every letter I wrote or received. He even had hidden cameras installed all over the common areas employees worked and socialized in. Naturally, all his woes were caused by the Jews, their plots against him, and their decades-long "persecution" of him.

'In a nutshell, Ernst wants to punish all the nations that, as he puts it, "bombed Germany into the Stone Age" and forced his Motherland to pay billions in reparations to the despised Jews. He wants to restore the reputation of Adolf Hitler, and usher in a revival of National Socialism. Everything he says, writes, broadcasts and does in his personal life is geared towards accomplishing those goals.'

Such are the beliefs and world view of the men—and they are nearly always men—trying to capitalize on the pain of the Middle East today. Never again, the world once said. That hope now looks increasingly fragile.

Holocaust denial is of course a spit in the face of victims of the Nazi genocide and their descendants. It serves to minimize the stigma associated with fascism and Nazi ideology so that the

Far Right can regain credibility in the public eye. By purporting to be academics merely 'seeking the truth' about the Holocaust, such revisionists shroud their antisemitism in a veneer of respectability. There are those, however, who refuse to stand by and do nothing while history is distorted.

Deborah Lipstadt's *Denying the Holocaust* provoked a libel suit by infamous British revisionist David Irving in the early 1990s. The case, in which by British law Lipstadt had the burden of proof, resulted in the judge vindicating Lipstadt, accepting as incontrovertible that the Holocaust did happen, and declaring Irving a bonafide Holocaust denier and antisemite.

As Lipstadt warns: 'We must function as canaries in the mine once did, to guard against the spread of noxious fumes. We must vigilantly stand watch against an increasingly nimble enemy. But unlike the canary, we must not sit silently by waiting to expire so that others will be warned of the danger. When we witness assaults on truth, our response must be strong, though neither polemical nor emotional. We must educate the broader public and academia about this threat and its historical and ideological roots. We must expose these people for what they are.'

VIEWPOINT 6

A Holocaust Denier Loses in Court
Douglas Davis

In the late 1990s, David Irving, a British writer with a solid reputation as a mainstream military historian, sued American scholar Deborah Lipstadt for libel in a British court. Irving claimed that Lipstadt had greatly harmed his reputation by calling him a Holocaust denier in a 1994 book. After a long case, the court affirmed that Irving was, indeed, a denier and that, therefore, no libel took place. Journalist Douglas Davis reports on the reaction to the verdict in the following article. Given Irving's status as a well-known and previously respected scholar and writer, the verdict was a noteworthy strike against the continuing problem of Holocaust denial. Douglas Davis writes articles for many publications and is the coauthor of A New Anti-Semitism? *and* Israel in the World: Changing Lives Through Innovation.

For much of the past five years, Deborah Lipstadt, an American Holocaust scholar, and David Irving, a British Holocaust denier, have been locked in a grotesque legal embrace. That close

Douglas Davis, "Irving Loses, but Lipstadt Says 'Nightmare Not Over,'" jweekly.com, Jewish Telegraphic Agency, April 14 2000. Copyright © 2000 by Jewish Telegraphic Agency. All rights reserved. Reproduced by permission. The article may not be reproduced without permission from JTA. For more information about JTA, please visit http://www.jta.org. If you would like to receive your FREE subscription to JTA's Daily Briefing, sign up at http://www.jta.org/briefing/index.htm.

encounter finally ended in the British High Court Tuesday [April 2000], when Justice Charles Gray ruled that Lipstadt was right when she labeled Irving a Holocaust denier.

Reaction to the verdict was swift and positive. "There no doubt were heartfelt sighs of deep relief in the offices of Jewish organizations worldwide," Efraim Zuroff, the director of the Simon Wiesenthal Center in Israel, wrote in a column for the Jerusalem Post.

After the judgment, Lipstadt, who is a professor at Emory University in Atlanta, said she was filled with intense joy and deep gratitude.

"I see this not only as a personal victory but also as a victory for all those who speak out against hate and prejudice," she said.

"But the nightmare is not over," she warned. "There is no end to the battle against racism, anti-Semitism and fascism."

Sure enough, shortly after the verdict was announced, the *Tehran Times* praised Irving, calling the Holocaust "one of the biggest frauds of the outgoing century" and accusing "Zionists" of making it up "to blackmail the West."

And a day after losing the suit, Irving used his Web site to accuse rich Jews, including the Bronfman family, of bankrolling Lipstadt's defense.

A spokesman for Edgar Bronfman, president of the World Jewish Congress, told Reuters he hoped his family had indeed contributed, saying, "I can't think of a more worthy defense fund."

Omer Bartov, a history professor at Rutgers University in New Jersey, said the verdict was significant because Irving has been seen by some as a serious historian with a treasure trove of documents on Hitler and other Nazis.

Formerly Respectable

Bartov said it was important to expose people like Irving, "who has been published by respectable publishers and been cited by scholars like me. But in recent years, he'd become more extreme, and associated himself with neo-Nazi circles."

Michael Berenbaum, professor of Holocaust studies at Clark University in Massachusetts, also said it is important for the court to help set professional standards for historians.

"Instead of going down into the gutter with Irving, we elevated the question into what is the obligation of a historian to interpret evidence and translate material. And Irving was found wanting," said Berenbaum, a former director of research at the U.S. Holocaust Memorial Museum in Washington.

"In a way, Holocaust denial has been defeated over and over and over again," he said, citing museums and movies and the public apologies of governments.

"What can you say about these guys who say the Holocaust never happened? They're a fringe movement of charlatans."

In a scathing 334-page judgment, Gray ruled that Lipstadt had proved the central charges she had leveled against Irving in her 1994 book, "Denying the Holocaust: The Growing Assault on Truth and Memory."

In the libel trial, Irving accused Lipstadt and her publisher of ruining his career by labeling him a Holocaust denier. The judge also exonerated her publisher, Penguin Books.

The judge did not mince words when he labeled Irving a "pro-Nazi polemicist" and found that he:

- Deliberately misrepresented and manipulated historical evidence to suit his own ideological agenda.
- Unjustifiably portrayed Hitler in a favorable light, particularly in his attitude toward, and treatment of, Jews.
- Associates with right-wing extremists who promote neo-Nazism.
- Is an anti-Semite, a racist and a Holocaust denier.

Referring to Irving's political activities, the judge said, "The content of his speeches and interviews often display a distinctly pro-Nazi and anti-Jewish bias."

Gray found that "for the most part, the falsification of the historical record was deliberate."

Irving presented events in a manner consistent with his own ideological beliefs, the judge said, and "makes surprising and often unfounded assertions about the Nazi regime which tend to exonerate the Nazis for the appalling atrocities they inflicted on the Jews."

The judge ruled that Lipstadt had failed to prove some of her claims about Irving, including that he has a self-portrait of Hitler above his desk.

But he added that the unproved charges would not have "any material effect on Irving's reputation."

Irving, who lives in a $1.5 million apartment in London's tony Mayfair district, now faces a bill for legal costs estimated to be $5 million. He claims no other assets besides his apartment and might have to file for bankruptcy.

Pelted with eggs as he entered the court building Tuesday [April 2000], Irving said after the verdict that he would not be silenced.

"I will still continue to write what I find to be true history. I can't be intimidated," Irving told Sky television.

Lipstadt said she regrets that Holocaust survivors attending the 32-day trial were forced to endure Irving's taunts.

Praise for the Verdict

Jewish groups from all political and religious viewpoints universally praised the ruling.

"Irving tried to manipulate the British legal system in order to put the victims murdered in the gas chambers on trial," the Simon Wiesenthal Center said in a statement. "Instead, the net result is that he will be relegated to the garbage heap of history's haters."

Abraham Foxman, the director of the Anti-Defamation League, cheered the ruling but expressed dismay that the trial ever took place.

"It is unfortunate that David Irving was able even to bring such frivolous charges into a courtroom," he said. "At least the trial provided an opportunity to reveal once again the reality of the Holocaust and the dangers of those who seek to deny it or trivialize it."

Said Sara Bloomfield, director of the Holocaust Memorial Museum in Washington, "The facts of the Holocaust are the facts. We didn't need a trial to prove that the Holocaust happened."

She bemoaned the fact that Lipstadt "had to take months out of her life and her scholarly work" to deal with Irving's lawsuit.

Bartov admitted that he hadn't closely followed the trial.

"Personally, I'm rather ambivalent about the whole public debate about Holocaust denial," he said. "It's a rather marginal phenomenon, and most of the people who use this rhetoric are marginal people.

"Arguments that there were no gas chambers at Auschwitz are for cranks," he said, adding that trials such as this one place "cranks in the center of a public debate rather than where they belong, which is at the margins."

Still, the debate will likely continue, Zuroff asserted in his column.

"The bad news is that the verdict will not finally put an end to Holocaust denial.

"The Holocaust deniers, after all, have been consistently manipulating the various historical facts and ignoring others for decades, and no antidote prepared by anybody has yet been found to stop this phenomenon."

CHAPTER 3

Personal Narratives

Chapter Exercises

1. **Writing Prompt**

   Imagine that you are a Jewish person who has just been ordered to board a train to a mysterious destination along with family and friends. Having heard rumors (that you hesitate to believe) that such trains might lead to slave labor or death camps, write a one-page diary entry examining your thoughts.

2. **Group Activity**

   Form groups and come up with five interview questions you could use to write oral histories of Holocaust survivors. Questions might consider their lives in ghettos or camps, their capture, and even some of the things that might have helped them to survive.

Viewpoint 1

A Survivor Recounts His Capture and His Journey to the Auschwitz Extermination Camp

Primo Levi

The following viewpoint was taken from author Primo Levi's Survival in Auschwitz. *Published in 1958, this book was among the first of the significant "survivors' accounts." In it, Levi writes of his capture in late 1943 by Italian fighters loyal to Adolf Hitler (and the then-deposed Italian dictator Benito Mussolini), and of the appearance of German troops in the prison camp where he was sent. He also writes of the steady loss of hope he and his fellow prisoners felt as they were sent by train to Auschwitz, where very few were chosen to be kept alive—to serve as slave workers. Primo Levi worked as a chemist following his liberation from Auschwitz and has authored several books, including* The Periodic Table *and* The Drowned and the Saved.

I was captured by the Fascist Militia [Italians allied to Nazi Germany] on 13 December 1943....

At that time I had not yet been taught the doctrine I was later to learn so hurriedly in the Lager [a Nazi camp]: that man is bound to pursue his own ends by all possible means, while he who errs but once pays dearly. So that I can only consider the

Primo Levi, "The Journey," from *If This Is a Man (Survival in Auschwitz)*, trans. Stuart Woolf. Translation copyright © 1959 by Orion Press, Inc., ©1958 by Giulio Einaudi editore S.P.A. Used by permission of Viking Penguin, a division of Penguin Group (USA) LLC.

following sequence of events justified. Three Fascist Militia companies, which had set out in the night to surprise a much more powerful and dangerous band than ours, broke into our refuge one spectral snowy dawn and took me down to the valley as a suspect person.

During the interrogations that followed, I preferred to admit my status of 'Italian citizen of Jewish race'. I felt that otherwise I would be unable to justify my presence in places too secluded even for an evacuee; while I believed (wrongly as was subsequently seen) that the admission of my political activity would have meant torture and certain death. As a Jew, I was sent to Fossoli, near Modena, where a vast detention camp, originally meant for English and American prisoners-of-war, collected all the numerous categories of people not approved of by the newborn Fascist Republic.

At the moment of my arrival, that is, at the end of January 1944, there were about one hundred and fifty Italian Jews in the camp, but within a few weeks their number rose to over six hundred. For the most part they consisted of entire families captured by the Fascists or Nazis through their imprudence or following secret accusations. A few had given themselves up spontaneously, reduced to desperation by the vagabond life, or because they lacked the means to survive, or to avoid separation from a captured relation, or even—absurdly—'to be in conformity with the law'. There were also about a hundred Jugoslavian military internees and a few other foreigners who were politically suspect.

The arrival of a squad of German SS [Schutzstaffel] men should have made even the optimists doubtful; but we still managed to interpret the novelty in various ways without drawing the most obvious conclusions. Thus, despite everything, the announcement of the deportation caught us all unawares.

On 20 February, the Germans had inspected the camp with care and had publicly and loudly upbraided the Italian commissar for the defective organization of the kitchen service and for the scarce amount of wood distribution for heating; they even said that an infirmary would soon be opened. But on the morning of the 21st we learned that on the following day the Jews would be leaving. All the Jews, without exception. Even the children, even the old, even the ill. Our destination? Nobody knew. We should be prepared for a fortnight of travel. For every person missing at the roll-call, ten would be shot.

Only a minority of ingenuous and deluded souls continued to hope; we others had often spoken with the Polish and Croat refugees and we knew what departure meant.

For people condemned to death, tradition prescribes an austere ceremony, calculated to emphasize that all passions and anger have died down, and that the act of justice represents only a sad duty towards society which moves even the executioner to pity for the victim. Thus the condemned man is shielded from all external cares, he is granted solitude and, should he want it, spiritual comfort; in short, care is taken that he should feel around him neither hatred nor arbitrariness, only necessity and justice, and by means of punishment, pardon.

But to us this was not granted, for we were many and time was short. And in any case, what had we to repent, for what crime did we need pardon? The Italian commissar accordingly decreed that all services should continue to function until the final notice: the kitchens remained open, the corvées [work groups] for cleaning worked as usual, and even the teachers of the little school gave lessons until the evening, as on other days. But that evening the children were given no homework.

And night came, and it was such a night that one knew that human eyes would not witness it and survive. Everyone felt this: not one of the guards, neither Italian nor German, had the courage to come and see what men do when they know they have to die.

Preparing for Death

All took leave from life in the manner which most suited them. Some praying, some deliberately drunk, others lustfully intoxicated for the last time. But the mothers stayed up to prepare the food for the journey with tender care, and washed their children and packed the luggage; and at dawn the barbed wire was full of children's washing hung out in the wind to dry. Nor did they forget the diapers, the toys, the cushions and the hundred other small things which mothers remember and which children always need. Would you not do the same? If you and your child were going to be killed tomorrow, would you not give him to eat today?

In hut 6A old Gattegno lived with his wife and numerous children and grandchildren, his sons, and daughters-in-law. All the men were carpenters; they had come from Tripoli after many long journeys, and had always carried with them the tools of their trade, their kitchen utensils and their accordions and violins to play and dance to after the day's work. They were happy and pious folk. Their women were the first to silently and rapidly finish the preparations for the journey in order to have time for mourning. When all was ready, the food cooked, the bundles tied together, they unloosened their hair, took off their shoes, placed the Yahrzeit [Jewish ceremonial] candles on the ground and lit them according to the customs of their fathers, and sat on the bare soil in a circle for the lamentations, praying and weeping all the night. We collected in a group in front of their door, and we experienced within ourselves a grief that was new for us, the ancient grief of the people that [have] no land, the grief without hope of the exodus which is renewed every century. . . .

Setting Off

With the absurd precision to which we later had to accustom ourselves, the Germans held the roll-call. At the end the officer asked *'Wieviel Stück?'* ["How many pieces?"] The corporal saluted smartly and replied that there were six hundred and fifty 'pieces' and that all was in order. They then loaded us on to the buses and took us to the station of Carpi. Here the train was waiting for us, with our escort for the journey. Here we received the first blows: and it was so new and senseless that we felt no pain, neither in body nor in spirit. Only a profound amazement: how can one hit a man without anger?

There were twelve goods wagons for six hundred and fifty men; in mine we were only forty-five, but it was a small wagon. Here then, before our very eyes, under our very feet, was one of those notorious transport trains, those which never return, and of which, shuddering and always a little incredulous, we had so often heard [spoken]. Exactly like this, detail for detail: goods wagons closed from the outside, with men, women and children pressed together without pity, like cheap merchandise, for a journey towards nothingness, a journey down there, towards the bottom. This time it is us who are inside.

Sooner or later in life everyone discovers that perfect happiness is unrealizable, but there are few who pause to consider the antithesis: that perfect unhappiness is equally unattainable. The obstacles preventing the realization of both these extreme states are of the same nature: they derive from our human condition which is opposed to everything infinite. Our ever-insufficient knowledge of the future opposes it: and this is called, in the one instance, hope, and in the other, uncertainty of the following day. The certainty of death opposes it: for it places a limit on every joy, but also on every grief. The inevitable material cares oppose it: for as they poison every lasting happiness, they equally assiduously distract us from our misfortunes and make our consciousness of them intermittent and hence supportable.

It was the very discomfort, the blows, the cold, the thirst that kept us aloft in the void of bottomless despair, both during the journey and after. It was not the will to live, nor a conscious resignation; for few are the men capable of such resolution, and we were but a common sample of humanity.

The doors had been closed at once, but the train did not move until evening. We had learnt of our destination with relief. Auschwitz: a name without significance for us at that time, but it at least implied some place on this earth.

The Holocaust

The train travelled slowly, with long, unnerving halts. Through the slit we saw the tall pale cliffs of the Adige Valley and the names of the last Italian cities disappear behind us. We passed the Brenner [Pass, through the Alps] at midday of the second day and everyone stood up, but no one said a word. The thought of the return journey stuck in my heart, and I cruelly pictured to myself the inhuman joy of that other journey, with doors open, no one wanting to flee, and the first Italian names . . . and I looked around and wondered how many, among that poor human dust, would be struck by fate. Among the forty-five people in my wagon only four saw their homes again; and it was by far the most fortunate wagon.

We suffered from thirst and cold; at every stop we clamoured for water, or even a handful of snow, but we were rarely heard; the soldiers of the escort drove off anybody who tried to approach the convoy. Two young mothers, nursing their children, groaned night and day, begging for water. Our state of nervous tension made the hunger, exhaustion and lack of sleep seem less of a torment. But the hours of darkness were nightmares without end.

There are few men who know how to go to their deaths with dignity, and often they are not those whom one would expect. Few know how to remain silent and respect the silence of others. Our restless sleep was often interrupted by noisy and futile disputes, by curses, by kicks and blows blindly delivered to ward off some encroaching and inevitable contact. Then someone would light a candle, and its mournful flicker would reveal an obscure agitation, a human mass, extended across the floor, confused and continuous, sluggish and aching, rising here and there in sudden convulsions and immediately collapsing again in exhaustion.

Toward Auschwitz

Through the slit, known and unknown names of Austrian cities, Salzburg, Vienna, then Czech, finally Polish names. On the evening of the fourth day the cold became intense: the train ran through interminable black pine forests, climbing perceptibly.

The snow was high. It must have been a branch line as the stations were small and almost deserted. During the halts, no one tried any more to communicate with the outside world: we felt ourselves by now 'on the other side'. There was a long halt in open country. The train started up with extreme slowness, and the convoy stopped for the last time, in the dead of night, in the middle of a dark silent plain.

On both sides of the track rows of red and white lights appeared as far as the eye could see; but there was none of that confusion of sounds which betrays inhabited places even from a distance. By the wretched light of the last candle, with the rhythm of the wheels, with every human sound now silenced, we awaited what was to happen.

Next to me, crushed against me for the whole journey, there had been a woman. We had known each other for many years, and the misfortune had struck us together, but we knew little of each other. Now, in the hour of decision, we said to each other things that are never said among the living. We said farewell and it was short; everybody said farewell to life through his neighbour. We had no more fear.

Arrival

The climax came suddenly. The door opened with a crash, and the dark echoed with outlandish orders in that curt, barbaric barking of Germans in command which seems to give vent to a millennial anger. A vast platform appeared before us, lit up by reflectors. A little beyond it, a row of lorries. Then everything was silent again. Someone translated: we had to climb down with our luggage and deposit it alongside the train. In a moment the platform was swarming with shadows. But we were afraid to break that silence: everyone busied himself with his luggage, searched for someone else, called to somebody, but timidly, in a whisper.

A dozen SS men stood around, legs akimbo, with an indifferent air. At a certain moment they moved among us, and in a subdued tone of voice, with faces of stone, began to interrogate us rapidly, one by one, in bad Italian. They did not interrogate everybody, only a few: 'How old? Healthy or ill?' And on the basis of the reply they pointed in two different directions.

Everything was as silent as an aquarium, or as in certain dream sequences. We had expected something more apocalyptic: they seemed simple police agents. It was disconcerting and disarming. Someone dared to ask for his luggage: they replied, 'luggage afterwards'. Someone else did not want to leave his wife: they said, 'together again afterwards'. Many mothers did not want to be separated from their children: they said 'good, good, stay with child'. They behaved with the calm assurance of people doing their normal duty of every day. But Renzo stayed an instant too long to say good-bye to Francesca, his fiancée, and with a single blow they knocked him to the ground. It was their everyday duty.

In less than ten minutes all the fit men had been collected together in a group. What happened to the others, to the women, to the children, to the old men, we could establish neither then nor later: the night swallowed them up, purely and simply. Today, however, we know that in that rapid and summary choice each one of us had been judged capable or not of working usefully for the Reich; we know that of our convoy no more than ninety-six men and twenty-nine women entered the respective camps of Monowitz-Buna and Birkenau, and that of all the others, more than five hundred in number, not one was living two days later. We also know that not even this tenuous principle of discrimination between fit and unfit was always followed, and that later the simpler method was often adopted of merely opening both the doors of the wagon without warning or instructions to the new arrivals. Those who by chance climbed down on one side of the convoy entered the camp; the others went to the gas chamber.

This is the reason why three-year-old Emilia died: the historical necessity of killing the children of Jews was self-demonstrative to the Germans. Emilia, daughter of Aldo Levi of Milan, was a curious, ambitious, cheerful, intelligent child;

her parents had succeeded in washing her during the journey in the packed car in a tub with tepid water which the degenerate German engineer had allowed them to draw from the engine that was dragging us all to death.

Thus, in an instant, our women, our parents, our children disappeared. We saw them for a short while as an obscure mass at the other end of the platform; then we saw nothing more.

Viewpoint 2

Watching the Departure of Ghetto Children to One of Nazi Germany's Death Camps

Oscar Singer

Even before the Nazis began their large-scale massacres, they began to enclose Jewish people in overcrowded, disease-ridden ghettos in occupied Poland. There, Jews were governed by Jewish Councils made up of elders who served as intermediaries with Nazi authorities. Once the massacres began, the ghettos were steadily liquidated as groups of victims were deported to the death camps. In the following viewpoint, an observer writes of the process of deportation from the Polish city of Lodz, beginning in September 1942. The observer, a Czech named Oscar Singer, notes that the deportations were organized by elders (notably the president of the Jewish Council, Chaim Rumkowski), and that potential deportees understood what was in store for them. He also writes how many were desperate to save their children and themselves. Oscar Singer died in the ghetto in 1944.

On September 5 the situation became clearer, and the frightening whispers of the past days became terrifying fact. The evacuation of children and old people took on the shape of real-

"Notes by an Observer in the Lodz Ghetto Following the Deportation of the Children," *Documents on the Holocaust*, ed. Yitzhak Arad, Israel Gutman, and Abraham Margialot. Lincoln: University of Nebraska Press, 1999. Copyright © 1999 by Yad Vashem. Reproduced by permission of Yad Vashem Publications.

ity. A small piece of paper on the wall in a busy part of the city announced an address by the President in an urgent matter. A huge crowd in Fire Brigade Square. The "Jewish Elder" [the top Jewish official in the ghetto] will reveal the truth in the rumors. For it concerns the young, for whom he has great love, and the aged, for whom he has much respect. "It cannot be that they will tear the babes from their mothers' breasts, and drag old fathers and old mothers to some unknown place. The German is without mercy, he wages a terrible war, but he will not go as far as that in cruelty." Everybody has faith in the President [the "Elder"] and hopes for words of comfort from him.

The representative of the ghetto is speaking. His voice fails him, the words stick in his throat. His personal appearance also mirrors the tragedy. One thing was understood by everybody: 20,000 persons must leave the ghetto, children under 10 and old people over 65. . . .

Trying to Stay

Everybody is convinced that the Jews who are deported are taken to destruction. . . . People ran here and there, crazed by the desire to hide the beloved victims. But nobody knew who would direct the *Aktion*: the Jewish Police, the Gestapo in the ghetto, or a mobile unit of the SS [Schutzstaffel]. The President, in coordination with the German authorities, decided in his area of responsibility to carry out the deportation (with his own forces). It was the Jewish Police that had to tear the children from the mothers, to take the parents from their children. . . . It was to be expected that parents and relatives would try in this situation to make changes and corrections in registered ages. Errors and inaccuracies that had not been corrected up to now did exist. Something that gives you the right to live today may well decide your fate tomorrow. There was a tendency to raise the age of the children, because a child from the age of 10 up could go to work and so be entitled to a portion of soup. Other parents lowered the age, because a younger child had a prospect

Jewish children are deported from the Lodz ghetto to the Chelmno concentration camp in 1942 Poland. © Galerie Bilderwelt/Getty Images.

of getting milk. Yesterday the milk and the soup were the most important things, today there is literally a question of staying alive. The age of the old people also moved up and down for various reasons.

An unprecedented migration began to the Registration Office. The officials tried to manage the situation. They worked without stopping, day and night. The pressure of the people at the office windows increased all the time. The applicants yelled, wept and went wild. Every second could bring the death sentence, and hours passed in the struggle to restrain their passion . . . On Saturday the Gestapo already began on the operation [deportation], without paying any attention to the feverish work of registration that had been going on at No. 4 Church Square. Everyone had supposed that the Order Police [Jewish

Police] would not stand the test. It could not itself carry out the work of the hangmen. . . .

The little ones who were loaded on the cart behaved quietly, in submission, or yelling, according to their ages. The children of the ghetto, boys and girls less than 10 years old, are already mature and familiar with poverty and suffering. The young look around them with wide-open eyes and do not know what to do. They are on a cart for the first time in their lives, a cart that will be pulled by a real horse, a proper horse. They are looking forward to a gay ride. More than one of the little ones jumps for joy on the floor of the wagon as long as there is enough space. And at the same time his mother has almost gone out of her mind, twisting about on the ground and tearing the hair from her head in despair. It is difficult to overcome several thousand mothers. It is difficult to persuade them to give their children up willingly to death, as a sacrifice. It is difficult to take out the old people who hide in the smallest and most hidden corners.

All this was to be expected. The President imposed a general curfew which came into force at 5 o'clock on Sunday afternoon. Anyone who broke it was threatened with deportation.

VIEWPOINT 3

The Horrors of the Holocaust Included Medical Experiments on Young Prisoners

Zoe Johannsen

The following viewpoint consists of a brief 2010 interview conducted by Zoe Johannsen, an Illinois middle-school student. Her interviewee is Auschwitz survivor Eva Mozes Kor, who was deported to a Nazi death camp with five family members, including a twin sister. The twins' experiences included being used as subjects in medical experiments. Auschwitz maintained an extensive hospital wing where medical experiments were conducted using Jewish prisoners. The most notorious of the doctors who worked there was Josef Mengele, often called the "Angel of Death." Other survivors remember him as the one determining whether new arrivals would be sent away for labor or gassed immediately. Mengele was especially interested in examining pairs of children who were twins, thinking that by doing so he might find ways to strengthen German racial characteristics. Johannsen's interviewee and her sister were among the few to survive these medical experiments.

Some of history's most important lessons aren't found in textbooks. They are stored in the minds of ordinary people who

Zoe Johannsen, "I Will Survive: One Girl's Life in A Nazi Death Camp," *Current Events: A Weekly Reader Publication*, vol. 109, no. 25, May 10, 2010. From *Current Events*, May 10, 2010. Copyright © 2010 by The Weekly Reader Corporation. Reprinted by permission of the publisher.

have lived through extraordinary events. Eva Mozes Kor survived one of the most horrific events in history—the Holocaust, the systematic killing of millions of people labeled as inferior by the Nazis, a political party led by Adolf Hitler in Germany. About 6 million Jews died in the Holocaust, which occurred during World War II (1939–1945). In March 1944, soldiers rounded up Kor; her twin sister, Miriam; and their family from their small village in Romania and deported them to Auschwitz, the notorious concentration camp in Nazi-occupied Poland. Eva and Miriam were ripped from their family to join about 1,400 pairs of twins. Those twins would endure the torturous medical experiments of Josef Mengele, a German doctor.

Kor told her story to Zoe Johannsen, an eighth grader at Nichols Middle School in Evanston, [Illinois]. Zoe's entry is this year's [2010] Eyewitness to History Contest winner. Read on to find out how Kor survived.

Zoe Johannsen [ZJ]: How was your life different before and after Auschwitz?

Eva Kor [EK]: First of all, we lived in a very small village, a very peaceful village, [with] about a hundred families. [We lived] with my parents and two older sisters. After [arriving at Auschwitz] I didn't have a family. I didn't have food. I didn't have rights. There is no comparison. One is hell that you are trying to survive, and the other is life.

ZJ: What was Auschwitz like?

EK: Life was an every-moment challenge. Surviving was a full-time job—you could not let your guard down for one single moment. I stepped over dead bodies daily. Food was very, very little. . . . The conditions in the barracks were atrocious—filthy, crude. It was a modular horse barn converted into living quarters for inmates [with] three-story-high bunk beds infested with rats and mice.

ZJ: What happened to your family at Auschwitz?

The Holocaust

EK: Within 10 minutes, my father and two older sisters were gone. And my mother was ripped apart from us. Within 30 minutes, Miriam and I no longer had a family. . . . They were gone, disappeared from the face of this Earth.

ZJ: *What was it like knowing that your family may have died?*

EK: I did not know that they died when I was in Auschwitz. Nobody really knew. . . . Everything was a big, dark secret, and we did not know what was going on. . . . [Surviving] took up every ounce of energy that I had. I could not concentrate on my own survival and at the [same] time even think about my parents. . . . I always pushed it in the background because survival took up every ounce of energy I had as a child.

ZJ: *How did you feel after surviving Auschwitz?*

EK: I was extremely, extremely glad that I beat the odds and that Miriam and I did not end up on the filthy latrine floor. . . . We were 11 years old. We were still young after liberation. We had a lot of health problems. We had a lot of infections—skin infections. My teeth were in very bad shape. I had a lot of unexplainable problems that [were probably from malnutrition].

ZJ: *Do you remember any of Dr. Mengele's experiments? [Josef Mengele is the most commonly remembered Nazi doctor at Auschwitz.]*

EK: The experiments were two types. . . . On Monday, Wednesday, and Friday, they would . . . place us naked for six to eight hours. Most of the time we were standing; sometimes we were sitting along benches. Every part of my body was measured and compared to charts, compared to my twin sister. These experiments were not dangerous, but they were unbelievably demeaning. . . . The only way I could cope with it for that length of time was by blocking it out of my mind. Three times a week—on Tuesday, Thursday, and Saturday—they would take us to another lab that I called the blood lab. There, they would tie both of my arms, take a lot of my blood from my left arm, while at the same time giving

Personal Narratives

Photos of a prisoner being subjected to medical experiments are on display at the Sachsenhausen Memorial and Museum, a former concentration camp in Oranienburg, Germany. © Sven Kaestner/AP Images.

me . . . injections into my right arm. . . . After one of those injections, I became very ill, a fact I desperately tried to hide because the rumor in the camp was [that] anyone taken to the hospital never came back. . . . I was taken to the hospital [after] my next visit to the blood lab. They measured my fever [at the lab], and I knew I was in trouble, and I was taken to the hospital. The hospital in this case was barracks filled with three-story-high bunk beds, with people who were not able to move. They looked more dead than alive, and they were screaming [constantly]. I was placed in a small room with two twins . . . who told me that . . . people were brought here to die. The next morning, Dr. Mengele came in with four other doctors. He looked at my fever chart. . . . Then Dr. Mengele declared, laughing sarcastically . . . "Too bad she's so young. She has only two weeks to live."

I refused to die. I made a . . . silent pledge that I would prove Dr. Mengele wrong: I will survive and be reunited with my twin sister, Miriam.

Kor did survive, and so did her sister Miriam. They endured life in Auschwitz for nine months before Soviet troops liberated the camp on Jan. 27, 1945. After the war, Kor and her sister went home to Romania, which had come [under] trader strict Communist rule. In 1950, the twins immigrated to Israel, where Kor met her husband. In 1960, the couple moved to the United States to raise a family. Today, Kor runs the CANDLES (Children of Auschwitz Nazi Deadly Lab Experiments Survivors) Holocaust Museum and Education Center in Terre Haute, Ind. The museum strives "for the elimination of hatred and prejudice from our world."

VIEWPOINT 4

Surviving the Warsaw Ghetto, Auschwitz, and the Death Marches

Solomon Radasky

Polish Jew Solomon Radasky tells his story in the following viewpoint. Like many Polish survivors, Radasky's first experience of German oppression was being shut into a ghetto and watching his family dwindle. Eventually he was sent to Auschwitz where he was chosen for slave labor rather than immediate death. Radasky notes that he experienced both moments of brutality and even a few of kindness at the camp. Finally, and like a number of other survivors, Radasky was forced to accompany the Germans when they abandoned Auschwitz in January 1942. The subsequent "death marches" back to Germany in the middle of winter killed many, while those who survived ended up being dumped at one or another German labor or concentration camps as the nation collapsed in the final months of the war. Throughout his experiences, Radasky tried to keep his faith alive. He was liberated by American forces on May 1, 1945.

I am from Warsaw. I lived in Praga, which is the part of the city across the Vistula river. I had a nice life there; I had my own shop where I used to make fur coats. In Warsaw when a Jewish

Solomon Radasky, "Portrait of a Survivor: Solomon Radasky," holocaustsurvivors.org. Copyright © by John Menszer, project director of the Holocaust Survivors website. All rights reserved. Reproduced by permission.

holiday came we used to know it was a holiday. All the stores were closed, and the people were in the synagogues.

Out of the 78 people in my family, I am the only one to survive. My parents had 3 boys and 3 girls: My parents were Jacob and Toby; my brothers were Moishe and Baruch, and my sisters were Sarah, Rivka and Leah. They were all killed.

My mother and my older sister were killed in the last week of January 1941. The year 1941 was a cold winter with a lot of snow. One morning the SD [the security service that played an important role in carrying out the Final Solution] and the Jewish police caught me in the street. I was forced to work with a lot of other people clearing snow from the railroad tracks. Our job was to keep the trains running.

When I returned to the ghetto I found out that my mother and older sister had been killed. The Germans demanded that the Judenrat collect gold and furs from the people in the ghetto. When they asked my mother for jewelry and furs, she said she had none. So they shot her and my older sister too.

My father was killed in April 1942. He went to buy bread from the children who were smuggling food into the ghetto. The children brought bread, potatoes and cabbages across the wall into the Warsaw ghetto. A Jewish policeman pointed out my father to a German and told him that he saw my father take a bread from a boy at the wall. The German shot my father in the back.

Life in the Ghetto

The deportations started on July 22, 1942. My other 2 sisters and 2 brothers went to Treblinka. After that I never saw anybody from my family again.

I am a furrier. In the ghetto I worked at Tobbens' shop. We made lambs' wool jackets for the German army. These were short jackets; today we would call them Eisenhower jackets.

For lunch they gave us bread and soup. In the evening we got another bread and coffee. When Poles came to the shop, we could trade with them for extra food. We gave them a few shirts for a piece of salami and some bread or potatoes to make a soup. But how long could our situation last?

One day there was a selection and I was pulled from the shop. However, I was lucky because a Volksdeutscher [a Pole of German heritage] told them I was a good worker. So I was allowed to go back to the shop, and someone else was put in my place.

A friend told me that he saw one of my sisters working at Shultz's shop. I wanted to see her, but I was 3 kilometers away and I did not know how to get there. A Jewish policeman told me that he could get a German soldier to go with me and bring me back. It would cost 500 zlotys, which was a lot of money, but I said OK.

The soldier put me in handcuffs, and he walked behind me with a rifle like I was his prisoner. When I got to Shultz's shop, I could not find my sister. Then I found that I was stuck there. I could not go back because the ghetto had been surrounded by German soldiers. The next morning was April 19, 1943, which was the day the Warsaw Ghetto Uprising began.

On May 1, 1943, I was shot in the right ankle. The bullet went through the meat and not the bone, so I did not lose my leg. I was taken to the Umschlagplatz [the transfer point]. The Treblinka extermination camp could only take 10,000 people a day. In our group we were 20,000. They cut off half of our train and sent it to Majdanek concentration camp. Majdanek was another death camp.

At Majdanek they took our clothes and gave us striped shirts, pants and wooden shoes. I was sent to Barracks 21. As I lay in my bed, an older man asked me how I was. He said, "I can help you." He had been a doctor in Paris. He took a little pocket knife and operated on me. To this day I do not understand how he could have kept a knife in the camp. There were no medicines or bandages. He said, "I have no medication, you have to help yourself. When you urinate use some of the urine as an antiseptic on your wound."

The Holocaust

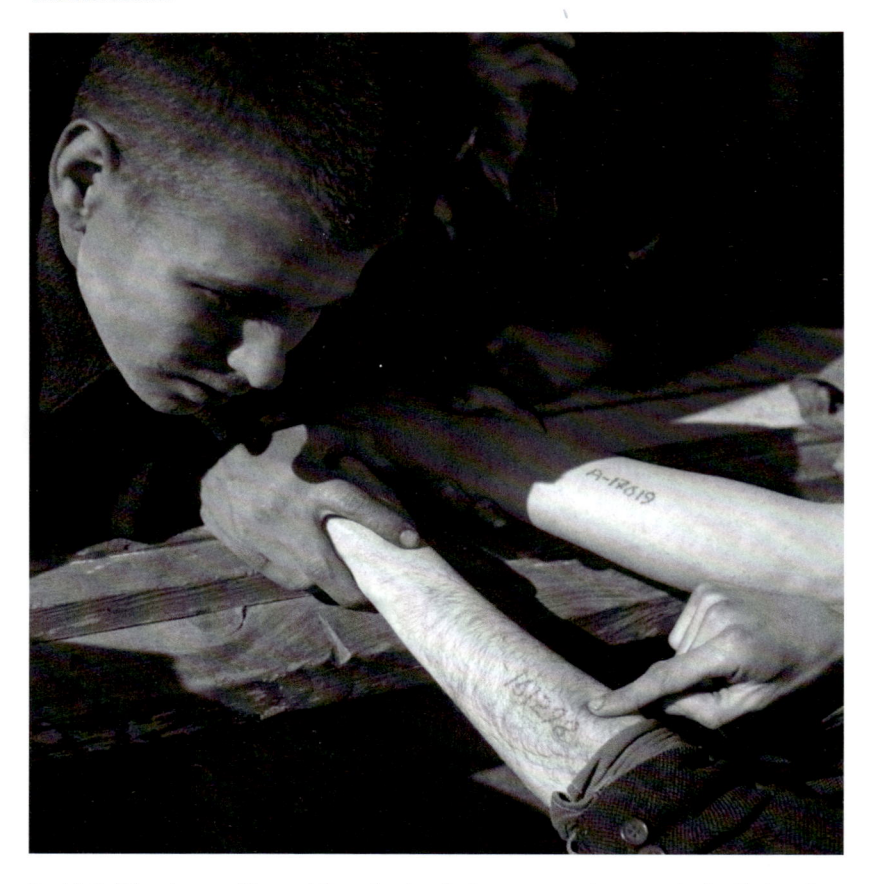

Jewish Polish prisoners liberated from the Auschwitz concentration camp in April 1945 show a young man the numbers tattooed by the Nazis on their arms. © Eric Schwab/AFP/Getty Images.

His First Death Camp

We had to walk 3 kilometers to work. I had to hold myself up straight without limping and walk out of the gate of the camp. I was scared. If I limped, they would take me out of line. At Majdanek they hung you for any little thing. I did not know how I would make it. God must have helped me, and I was lucky.

We stood at the appell [roll call] in our wooden shoes. Then when we got out of the gate we had to take off our wooden shoes and tie them over our shoulders with a piece of string. We had to walk to work barefoot. There were little stones on the road that cut into your skin and blood was running from the feet of many people. The work was dirty field work. After a few days some people could not take it anymore, and they fell down in the road. If they could not get up, they were shot where they lay. After work we had to carry the bodies back. If 1,000 went out to work, a 1,000 had to come back....

The soldier took us to the railroad tracks, he put us on a train and the next morning we left Majdanek. I had been there 9 weeks. We were on this train for two nights and a day with no food or water. In my 9 weeks at Majdanek I had not changed my shirt or washed myself. We were eaten up with lice, and many of us were swollen from hunger.

When we got off the train, we saw that we had arrived at Auschwitz. There was a selection and some of us were machine gunned in a field there. They did not take them to the gas chambers.

I was taken to get a number tattooed on my arm. I got Number 128232. The separate numbers add up to 18. In the Hebrew language the letters of the alphabet stand for numbers. The letters which stand for the number eighteen spell out the Hebrew word "Chai," which means life. After I was tattooed, I was given a potato.

I was first sent to the camp at Buna. After I got out of quarantine, I was put to work building railroad tracks. The Capo [a camp official] there was a murderer. I am short, and he would put a short man together with a tall man to carry twenty-foot lengths of iron. The tall man I worked with had to bend his knees.

At Auschwitz

One time I fell down and could not get up. The Capo started screaming and beating me, and he pulled me aside. There was a selection, and we had to take off our clothes and stand naked the whole night. The next morning a truck with a red cross came, and they pushed us into it, one on top of the other. We thought that they were going to take us to the gas chambers.

Instead, we were taken to the Auschwitz I camp. A Polish man came out of a building, and he asked us to call out our numbers. I said, "128232." He looked at a paper and asked my name? I said, "Szlama Radosinski," which is my name in Polish and doesn't sound like a Jewish name. He asked me where I was from. "Warsaw," I said. How long was I there? "I was raised there," I said.

He started to cuss me like I never heard before in my life. He pulled me out of the line and put me in a corner. He said, "Stay here." He brought me a piece of blanket to cover myself with. I was freezing, so he brought me inside the barracks.

I lay down. I did not know what was happening or what to think. A young guy came up to me and said, "I know you." I asked him, "Who are you?" He said his name was Erlich and that he knew me from Majdanek.

I asked him what this place was. He said it was the hospital barracks, Block 20. He told me, "It is very bad here. Dr. Mengele comes two times a week to make selections. But this is Tuesday and he will not come again this week. I will let you know what is going to happen." I had not eaten since Monday. He gave me a bread.

Erlich had been there 5 weeks. He had come from Majdanek to Auschwitz the same day as I did. Two of the doctors at the hospital knew his grandfather, who had been their rabbi in Cracow. They had hidden him from Dr. Mengele. Those doctors had tried to help hide Jewish people in Cracow. When the SS [Schutzstaffel] came, they killed the Jews they hid and took the doctors to Auschwitz. . . .

I was working for over a year with the boys at the same job, digging sand. Ten of us worked in the sand mine. There was a little guy from Breslau that we made our supervisor. He stood on top, and we were 20 feet down below. Every day we loaded up a wagon with the sand and pushed it 16 kilometers. That was 2 trips of 4 kilometers one way and 4 kilometers coming back—over 10 miles a day.

Twice a day we carried sand to Birkenau to cover the ashes of the dead. The sand was to cover the ashes that came from the crematoria. I did this for more than a year.

The ovens were on one side of the crematoria, and the ashes came out this side. The other side was where the gas chamber was. The Sonderkommando [a group of Jewish slaves], took the ashes out of the ovens. There were big holes for the ashes and we covered the ashes with sand.

I saw when the transports came. I saw the people who were going in, who to the right and who to the left. I saw who was going to the gas chambers. I saw the people going to the real showers, and I saw the people going to the gas. In August and September of 1944 I saw them throw living children into the crematorium. They would grab them by an arm and a leg and throw them in.

One Saturday, when we were working, we turned around and saw a soldier with a rifle, so we started to speed up. The soldier said, "Slow down; today is your Sabbath." He was a Hungarian, and he said, "Come to my barracks at 4 o'clock, and I will have something for you. I will put out a bucket with trash in it. Look under the trash, and you will find eleven pieces of bread." For two or three weeks he put out bread for us. He asked us to bring him money from Canada [a warehouse where Jewish goods were stored], which we did. He used to tell us the names of the Jewish holidays. One day he disappeared.

The Russians were pushing back the Germans at Stalingrad. Transports were coming from the Lodz ghetto. That is when we saw them grab the little children by the head and the leg and throw them into the crematoria alive. Then the Hungarian people were coming.

There was this group of young people who wanted to destroy the crematoria. There were four crematoria in Birkenau. The young girls worked at an ammunition factory, and they smuggled in explosives. One crematorium was destroyed. They hung 2 of the girls in front of us when we came back from work.

Life was going on. Every day was a different problem until January 18, 1945, when they began liquidating Auschwitz. On the 18th I left Auschwitz, and 9 days later the Russians liberated it. Those 7 days cost me 5 months.

The Death March

When we left, everybody had to get out of the barracks. I was walking the whole night with a rabbi from Sosnowiec. The Rabbi had come from Block 2, which was the tailor shop. I saw that the soldiers behind us were shooting the people who fell down. The Rabbi fell down in the road and this boy from Belgium and I held up the Rabbi between us and kept walking. We saw a sled pulled by a soldier, and we asked him if we could pull the sled with the Rabbi in it until morning.

The guys who lived in Block 2, the tailors' barracks, could get some of the gold and the diamonds that people had sewn into the linings of their clothes. They gave their block leader some gold and diamonds to let them hide the Rabbi in the barracks. They hid him in a closet that they had built in the wall. They put the Rabbi in the closet when they went out to roll call at 6 o'clock in the morning and took him out when they came back in the evening. Many times I went there at 5 o'clock in the morning to say Kaddish [a memorial prayer] for my parents with the Rabbi.

At daylight we came to a small town and the farmers let us stay in the stables. In the evening we had to get out. We walked to a railroad station. In two days the train brought us to Gross-Rosen camp [in western Poland]. I never saw the Rabbi again.

Gross-Rosen was murder. The guards walked around with iron pipes in their hands. They said, "We are going to help you; we are going to get you out of here." We were put in a shed with two thousand men. In the daytime we had to stand up, and at night we slept head to food. The only food we got was a slice of bread and a cup of coffee at night. I thought I was going to die there.

They walked us to the railroad station, and in 3 days we came to Dachau [in southern Germany]. The train ride was terrible;

the train pulled up and pulled back, up and back. We ate snow for water. A man was in there with his son who went crazy. The son grabbed the father by the neck and choked him to death. At Dachau there was a selection for the typhus blocks. I had a friend from Radom who was strong. He could have made it, but they put him in the typhus block.

I left Dachau on the 26th or the 27th of April, 1945. I was liberated on May 1st. During this time we were traveling on trains. We were in Tutzing and in Feldafing and in Garmisch [nearby towns]. There were big mountains there. One day they had us get out of the train, and we had to go up twenty feet to the other side of the mountain. Then the Germans set up machine guns and started to fire at us. A few hundred were killed as we ran back to the train.

Liberation

The next day we heard planes dropping bombs. A few hours later the soldiers opened the door to the train. They said they needed a few people to work cleaning up from the bombs, but we were scared to go. So they said, "You, you and you out," and they caught me. I said to myself, "I think this is the end. After all these years in the ghetto and losing everybody, now this is the end. Who is going to be left to say Kaddish for my family?"

We went to this small town on the other side of the mountain where the train station had been bombed. To one man they gave a shovel, to another a broom and to me they gave a pick. I saw a counter in the station where they were selling little black breads. I said to myself that I would like to eat a piece of bread before they kill me. I was ready for Kiddush Hashem [a Jewish ritual]. I grabbed a little dark bread into my jacket and started eating it. A soldier saw me and he howled, "Go to work." I stayed until I had eaten the bread. I did not move, even though he beat me. I fell down and he kicked me and I got up. I had to finish eating that little bread. Blood was running down my head. When I finished, I went to work. I had gotten my wish. Then I knew that I was going to survive.

Early at 4 A.M. the next morning near Tutzing we heard heavy traffic on the highway. We pushed to look out of the two little windows of the train. We expected to see the Russians coming but it was the Americans. We hollered. A jeep drove up with two soldiers. One was a short man, an MP. He spoke good German. He asked who we were. We said we were from the concentration camps. Everybody started hollering and crying. The American soldiers said we were free. They arrested the Germans and the Germans got scared. It was May 1, 1945.

VIEWPOINT 5

An American Jewish Woman, Originally from Hungary, Recalls Her Experiences

Leo Adam Biga

For much of World War II, the central European nation of Hungary was a German ally because the Soviet Union was its enemy. While Hungary remained an ally, its large Jewish population was almost entirely safe from the Holocaust—Adolf Hitler's minions unable to remove Jews due to the Hungarian government's refusal to cooperate. Then, in early 1944, Hungary's government was overthrown, and Nazi armies occupied the nation. The Schutzstaffel (SS), Hilter's paramilitary organization, soon followed, and their attempt to massacre Hungary's Jews was one of the last major killing initiatives at Auschwitz. In the following viewpoint, Holocaust survivor Kitty Williams tells her story to the Jewish Magazine's *Leo Adam Biga. She and her family suffered anti-Semitism, ghettoization, and, finally, deportation to Auschwitz. Williams was ultimately transferred to a munitions factory in Germany, where she was liberated by American forces in April 1945. She eventually married an American pilot and moved to the United States.*

Leo Adam Biga, "Holocaust Survivor Kitty Williams Tells Her Story," *Jewish Magazine*, January 2010. Originally published in the 2009 Jewish New Year's edition of the *Jewish Press*, a publication of the Jewish Federation of Omaha (Nebraska). Copyright © 2010 by Leo Adam Biga. All rights reserved. Reproduced by permission.

Born in 1924, Kitty grew up in the Eastern Hungarian town of Sarand, near the Rumanian border. She was the second youngest of eight siblings. Their father, Mor Ehrenfeld, was a World War I combat veteran who incurred wounds fighting in the Austro-Hungarian army. However, losing the mother of his children, his beloved wife Anna, cut deeper than any shrapnel.

"It changed everything," recalled Kitty. "It's almost like there was a life before my mother that was beautiful and there was a life after my mother died that was sad. Of course, my father took it very hard and really I don't think he ever recovered from the loss. He did not want to bring a step-mother into our lives. I remember he got us together and said, 'We'll make it, somehow we'll make it.'"

Kitty said, "I think most of all of the love that radiated between us is how we made it."

Her sister Magda, 12 years her senior, became Kitty's surrogate mother.

The family were the only Jews in the vicinity, except for the Leitners, whom they were not close to prior to the Holocaust. Circumstances would thrust the families together on a harrowing journey. Before the madness, Kitty recalls an idyllic life.

"I have beautiful memories mostly because of my large family. Most of my siblings were very musical and played instruments—that was our entertainment, sitting on the porch, my brothers playing these heartbreaking love songs on the violin. They're still etched in my memory. We were so close as family, and since socially we really weren't accepted in town, it was a wonderful feeling.

A Close Family

"We always had a lot of books in our house. We had probably the first radio—a crystal set. We got a newspaper from Budapest every day, although a day old."

Her father's 3rd grade education belied wisdom. He ran a general store in town, he dealt in grain, he owned a vineyard.

Harvest time marked a communal peasant celebration. "Half the town would come and pick the grapes," said Kitty. "It was kind of like 4th of July here. It was a get together for a lot of people."

Kitty said her father was admired for his advanced agricultural techniques and many skills.

"The school board approached him every year with different parcels of land for him to look at and he would farm these on shares . . . because he was always able to figure out what was needed, to build it up. The town didn't have a lawyer and so anytime anybody needed an official paper translated or written they would come to my dad. Besides, he had the most beautiful handwriting. For any advice there would be a knock on the window or on the door or somebody wanting, you know, 'My child is sick, can I have something from the store?'"

She said she's read *Who's Who in Hungary* listings praising him as a patriot, citing his WWI service. His community standing helped insulate the family from punitive, restrictive Jewish laws. Even when new, harsher anti-Jewish decrees began being instituted in 1939, she said, "he was always exempted from the Jewish laws until the very end." Nothing could save the family once German forces occupied Hungary, a noncombatant but complicit ally of the Nazi regime and its master race ideology. Up until then, Hungarian Jews and gypsies largely avoided the mass internments and killings. But as these ethnic minorities discovered to their horror many of Hungary's Christian leaders and citizens willingly participated in genocide. . . .

By 1939, the circle of Kitty's life narrowed. She was 15 and her family was dispersed, her older siblings married and moved away. It was just Kitty and her father. Back home in Sarand and in the nearby city of Debrecen, where Kitty attended high school and her sister Magda lived, things were getting more difficult.

"I was a young girl but I couldn't get out except maybe for a couple hours a day. You couldn't travel, you were forbidden to do anything."

Wearing the Star of David in public became compulsory. Once, when a Gentile [non-Jewish] girl asked her to go to the movies, Kitty, anxious to leave the house and be a normal teenager again, agreed. "It was like a dream to get out of my almost virtual prison." The dream turned nightmare. The movie was a virulent German propaganda film. Walking home from the theater in the chill of the afternoon Kitty put on a coat, covering her Yellow Star. Someone must have reported her, as the next day the police came to her home and arrested her. She was taken away and jailed in another town despite the protests and pleadings of her and her father.

"I just begged and begged, 'I have to be with my dad, please let me out,' but they had no mercy. They kept me in there."

She got out only after a Gentile woman who once worked for the family walked the 8 kilometers to obtain her release. Kitty suspects her father gave the woman money to bribe officials. Kitty will never know though as the incident "was never discussed." Kitty's father had been allowed to keep his store but eventually he was forced to close it. Then, on March 19, 1944, the German Army occupied Hungary.

"I remember I was visiting my sister Magda in Debrecen. She was married and pregnant. I was walking on the street and I saw German troops marching all over. They'd just landed or drove into Hungary. It happened all in one day. They just descended on us. They were everywhere. That's when we became very scared."

"Even to Go to Our Death It Was Torture"

Before long her brothers were nabbed and sent to forced labor camps. Her sister Elizabeth, who lived in the capital city Budapest, was taken prisoner the very day the Germans stormed into Hungary. She ended up in Auschwitz with Kitty and Magda. Another sister, Klari, was forced from her home in Budapest to march with thousands of others. Their supposed destination—Vienna. But standing orders said no Jews were to make it there alive. Stragglers or resistors were shot on the spot.

Klari was a comely young woman who, with a girlfriend, drew the attention of a Hungarian guard. He confided they would not survive the march and offered to hide them at his family's home in Budapest. Klari accepted the offer and lived. Her girlfriend refused and died. Klari ended up a virtual slave but she made it through.

It was awhile before the Germans reached Kitty's town. She can never forget the mob that came for her in the middle of the night. Rape and murder on their minds.

"The first night we heard . . . let me put it this way, we had our Kristallnacht. It was a mixture of German and Hungarian hoodlums. They broke every window in the house. My dad got up. The Germans demanded I come out. They wanted me. I was a young girl of not even 19. Fortunately my dad spoke German. He said, 'I'm so sorry, she's not here.' The Hungarians were more demanding."

Somehow he convinced the thugs she wasn't there. They left uttering epithets. "I remember spending the night under the bed shaking," said Kitty, "and from then on I never slept at home." For a time she hid in the apartment of a Christian family in Debrecen. But the stress of avoiding detection became too much and the family put her out. Kitty wanted to be home anyway. "I didn't really like this hiding. I wanted to go and be with my dad, to take care of him." Her law-abiding father also wanted her home. He arranged for her to travel in the wagon of a farmer going to market. Posing as a Gentile, head wrapped in a babushka [thick scarf], she passed. . . .

In April the roundup of Jews began. Kitty's large home was designated a ghetto. Mr. and Mrs. Leitner and daughter Ica were taken there. The girls became friends. A doctor's widow, Mrs. Kovacs, was brought there, too. Only part Jewish, she'd lived as a Christian. "She came with all her furs and jewelry and she kept saying, 'I believe in Jesus Christ, how can this happen to me?' But, you know, it didn't matter," said Kitty. "If they knew you had even an ounce of Jewish blood. . . ."

Kitty and Ica were ordered into evacuated outlying ghettos, with an armed guard escort, to forage for food left behind. "That's how we supplied the camp," said Kitty. "We went from house to house and picked up food left here and there. The sight of it, it still chills me, because I would see children's things, a shoe here, a shoe there, toys, furniture, clothes. It looked like they must have been taken in the middle of the night and that they weren't prepared for it." She couldn't shake the scene of quiet lives so violently interrupted.

Weeks passed. Rumors of death camps and gas chambers spread. As did counter rumors the Germans needed the Jews for war labor. Kitty, her father and most others chose to believe their lives were too precious to be snuffed out. They were even hoping the railroad tracks that ran nearby would soon bring a train to transport them to a labor camp. Anything would be better than this, they thought. "You can't imagine the brutality from the Hungarians," said Kitty.

Deportation Horrors Came Next

It was "a relief" when a train did come for them in August. Relief gave way to dread as they were herded onto the cattle cars in the summer heat. "The horror of that I can't even . . ." she said, her voice breaking. "It's very hard for anybody in the free world to imagine what they did to us. Anything you've seen or read, it was much worse. They put us in there on top of each other with no water and a bucket for a toilet. We could never lie down. You couldn't see out. Total darkness. Just one little hole. And by this time we hardly had any food."

No one knew the destination. The journey was interminable, impossible, awful. "It seemed to me like it was at least five days," said Kitty. "I do know you can get there overnight by train." She refers to Auschwitz-Birkenau, the death camp they were en route to. It's a trip she's remade twice in the ensuing years. Getting there that first time was like a slow, agonizing death. "We stopped and slowed down, again and again.

It was like torture on purpose, even to go to our death it was torture." . . .

"We arrived early morning, the sun was just coming up. Nobody spoke to you, everybody yelled, they always yelled. 'Get out, get out! Leave your luggage, you'll get it later! Stand in line!' In the distance I saw this beautiful, tall German officer all in white with several dogs and soldiers around. He was sitting and looking at us, pointing—right, left. I found out later it was Dr. (Josef) Mengele." The selection separated Kitty from her father. "I went to the right with my friend and her parents and my dad went to the left." Kitty asked men in striped garb where the others were being taken. The cryptic reply: "You'll see." She learned "the striped ones were inmates who had the job of getting us organized. Everything was so organized. The method was so perfect. There were typists, barbers." Lines and names and counts. Chilling efficiency. Always, guns, whips, clubs at the ready.

Before her father was led away, she recalls embracing him, "looking over and saying something like, 'See you later.' Well, later never came. That was the last sight of him I ever had." She learned he was killed that same day. Her sister Elizabeth, who arrived before, was on a work detail sifting through clothes of those killed in the gas chambers. "It was," said Kitty, "a plum job. You would give your right arm for it because you were able to go through pockets and find food." A friend was rifling through a man's overcoat when she found a wedding picture she recognized as Elizabeth's. The overcoat belonged to Mor. He'd carried the photo with him. "That's how Elizabeth knew our father was dead. I have the picture."

The dead at least were free of degradation. The living had to endure more misery. In Kitty's experience, the worst brutality was meted out not by Germans but arm-banded kapos, prisoners working for the Nazis.

"They were so hardened by then. They'd been in concentration camps for years and seen so much that they weren't even like

The Holocaust

human beings anymore. Whatever beatings I had in the camp were always from a kapo."

A gray pall hung over this killing zone. "I don't think a blade of grass ever grew and I don't think a bird ever flew in Auschwitz. It was the most devastating place. It was death and smoke and smell. When it rained, it was mud. It was unbelievable.

"A Reason to Live"

Kitty said she was still "in denial" even with the crematoriums going full blast, the flames licking the sky, the stench of human flesh permeating the air. "I didn't want to face it. I could not believe it." The kapos didn't mince words when asked, "When will we see our parents?' The cold answer: "They're up in the smoke."

Stripped, shaved, showered, disinfected, the inmates got mismatched rags as clothes, a metal pan as a pillow. The newly built barrack or lager she and Ica were assigned was within a half-block of a crematorium. The barrack was a windowless barn with a dirt floor. No partitions. Approaching it, she said, "We saw these shaven heads atop walking skeletons. They were inquiring where we were from and did we know so-and-so." She passed another lager whose inmates "were even in worse shape. They were dark-skinned and there were entire families together." The identities of these exotics puzzled Kitty until learning they were gypsies.

"The first night was my introduction to seeing somebody dying. Somebody next to me had a diabetic reaction and died."

Death became numbingly routine. With no bunks, people were "half way on top of each other—a thousand of us in this one huge barrack. We were there a few days and new transports were coming from Hungary almost daily. The Germans were in a rush to kill us. They couldn't do it fast enough."

"August 2nd, 1944 we woke-up to this horrible noise, people begging for help. We went outside and saw smoke and flames from the crematorium chimney near us. Next to the crematorium was a ditch and from that direction there were screams and flames going up, the smell of human flesh burning. And that screaming, sometimes I wake up and it comes back to me. It just pierces to your soul."

When Kitty learned her sister Magda was in camp she managed finding her in another barrack. Magda had been expecting while in the Debrecen ghetto and so Kitty anticipated meeting the newborn, but there was no baby. It died in the ghetto. Unburied. Magda was desolate and weak. Kitty became her caregiver. "I fought for her to get even a drip of water, anything, because she really didn't have the strength. I moved over to her barrack. They kept track of us but not to the point where it made any difference because people were dying constantly." Kitty begged Ica to come with her but [she] declined. One day Kitty went to her old barrack to check on Ica and it was empty. The Germans had liquidated it.

Getting Magda back to a semblance of health gave Kitty "a reason to live. We were together." In mid August the sisters were fortunate to be selected for forced labor. Before boarding the train the Germans made a second cut, eliminating the sick. When a guard noticed Magda's lactating breasts she was pulled from the line.

"I was just devastated," said Kitty. "I was sure she would never make it. Neither of us could run back to the other without getting shot. She ended up with a lot worse fate than I did, but she did make it. She died a year ago at 96."

"We Were Just Happy to Get Out"

A book written by a camp mate of Kitty's reveals that male workers had been requested. Either due to lack of able-bodied men or a mix-up, said Kitty, "us girls" ended up in Allendorf, Germany. 1,000 of them. "We were just happy to get out," she said. By war's end, virtually all the women survived. Everything about Allendorf was an improvement over Auschwitz. Training in, the cattle cars were far less crowded. Kitty recalls her surprise looking out and seeing ordinary people going about their daily lives. "Life goes on on the outside? Not everybody is like us?"

A Lucky Mistake

The women's quarters were in the woods, the barracks built for free workers and "so it was not unbearable," said Kitty. The munitions factory was an hour's walk. "The work was heavy, it wasn't designed for females. My work was to chisel powder out of dud (undetonated) bombs, shells, grenades. Other people were filling them and putting them on the conveyor belt. The Germans were so desperate for war materials they were remixing, reusing explosives. It was a tremendous operation."

The workers handled toxic chemicals without protection—no gloves, no masks. The poison made people sick. Hair turned purple. Skin assumed a yellow cast. Shifts lasted 12 hours. The factory operated around the clock. The workers were issued wooden shoes and coming back and forth from the factory to camp the women clopped, clopped on the town's cobblestone streets.

Supervising were mostly civilian German overseers. Kitty described them as "more neutral" and "not really brutal." The few guards were mostly women and, she said, they "were particularly cruel. They punished us for just petty things." One German woman, however, did befriend Kitty and even though they couldn't speak each other's language a weakened Kitty was allowed respites from work at a forest hideaway. The German gave her extra food Kitty then shared with camp mates.

The prisoners heard snatches of news about the war's progress: the Allies landing, the war going badly for Germany. "But we didn't believe it," said Kitty. By March '45 food was scarce for everyone. In late March the commandant gathered the camp's entire contingent in a courtyard to announce he and his staff were leaving. The Americans were approaching. The war was over. "He told us, 'You're free to go, you're on your own. Good luck,'" Kitty said. It was a shock. Some survivors followed the commander and his staff. Most hit the road in groups. Kitty was among a group of 20 women who'd shared a room and become like sisters.

The Americans Arrive

"We decided to stick together. We went one direction. We had no idea really. We ate anything we could find—grass, vegetables in the fields, eggs in hen houses. We feared knocking on the doors of German houses. We were afraid of the reception we would get. Once in a while some of us, probably not me, [were] brave enough to knock. There was hostility from some, generosity from others."

One day on the road someone in Kitty's group spied a convoy of U.S. tanks. She took off her white slip, tied it to tree branch and flagged them down. It was April 1, 1945. Mor's birthday. The G.I.s became the survivors' liberators. "They showered us with candy and gum. I'd never had chewing gum. The Americans were almost childlike, so good, so unspoiled. They were like angels that dropped down from heaven," Kitty recalled. She and the others were trucked to the nearest village, whose burgomeister [master of the town] was pressed into putting them up, the villagers ordered to wait on them hand and foot. G.I.s stood guard to prevent reprisals. After a few days the Army decided it wasn't safe and relocated the women to Fritzlar, a former Luftwaffe air base. The women were offered housing, food, jobs, protection. They readily accepted. For two years Kitty lived and worked there, first as a mess hall waitress, then, having quickly picked up English, as a PBX [telephone switchboard] operator. Affairs and romances between G.I.s and native girls were common. Kitty was not immune.

VIEWPOINT 6

A Soldier Remembers the Liberation of One of Hitler's Camps

Phil Davison

It was not until the last months of World War II that Allied troops began to reach Hitler's camps. Their accounts, as well as those of medical personnel, journalists, and other observers quickly revealed the scale and methods of the Nazi genocide to a shocked world. Russian soldiers first liberated the prisoners of the Majdanek death camp in July 1944, then the Auschwitz prisoners in January 1945. The first of the major camps to be liberated by one of the Western Allies, Great Britain or the United States, was Bergen-Belsen in northwestern Germany. Already a vast labor and prison camp, Bergen-Belsen was one of the locations where a number of surviving Auschwitz prisoners were simply abandoned as the war came to an end. The following viewpoint, an obituary of Fred Smith, one of the British troopers who entered Belsen, offers an eyewitness account of what was found there.

During a local truce on 15 April 1945 after fierce fighting along the Rhine, Trooper Fred Smith, one of Montgomery's "Desert Rats" who had fought through North Africa and later Normandy, thought he had seen all the horrors of war. Hitler's

Phil Davison, "Trooper Fred Smith: Soldier Who Helped Liberate Bergen-Belsen," *The Independent*, July 1, 2011. Copyright © 2011 by Independent Print Ltd. All rights reserved. Reproduced by permission.

Personal Narratives

men were on the run, Smith's 7th Armoured Division were pushing towards Hamburg and Berlin and he was confident he'd soon be back in London's East End.

But that day was to change his life. After the Germans had asked for the truce, he was sent into a concentration camp, near the town of Celle in Lower Saxony, which became known as Bergen-Belsen. There, he encountered hell on earth. A reconnaissance patrol from the 1st Special Air Service (SAS) had gone into the camp first—to free a POW from the regiment—but quickly moved on. It was left to the British 11th Armoured Division and a unit of Canadian allies to liberate the camp before men of the 7th were sent in to help deal with the thousands of dead and dying inmates, many of them Jews but many of them Soviet or other prisoners of war. The Germans had asked for the truce because they feared rampant typhus in the camp, which had killed at least 35,000 inmates, could spread to their troops and (they added to make their point) to the advancing allied forces.

Smith later said: "Approaching Belsen, we knew immediately something was not right. I'd been on many battlefields and I knew this was the smell of death. We asked the local German civilians what had happened but they were in complete and utter denial."

He and his comrades found some 60,000 inmates, most of them seriously ill, but also 13,000 unburied corpses. "You could hardly tell who was alive and who was dead," Smith said. "We were afraid to lift people up in case they fell apart." One of those who had died only weeks before the liberation was Anne Frank, whose diary would eventually move the world.

The great BBC correspondent Richard Dimbleby, who was with the liberating troops, famously reported on radio: "Here over an acre of ground lay dead and dying people. You could not see which was which. The living lay with their heads against the corpses and around them moved the awful, ghostly procession of emaciated, aimless people, with nothing to do and with no hope of life. . . . Babies had been born here, tiny wizened things that could not live . . . This day at Belsen was the most horrible of my life."

Smith and his British comrades quarantined the camp, buried the dead in mass graves and tried to save the living by fumigating and feeding them before moving them to a nearby evacuated German Wehrmacht barracks for further treatment. The Brits gave the survivors their bully beef from army rations, skimmed milk and what they called Bengal Famine Mixture, based on rice and sugar, but these proved too rich for the starving inmates. In spite of the British troops' efforts, more than 13,000 more Belsen inmates died in the weeks after the camp's liberation.

"Because the German civilians in nearby towns were still in denial, we took them to the camp to see what had happened," Trooper Smith recalled. The arrival of a Jewish British army chaplain, the Welsh Rev Leslie Hardman . . . two days after the liberation, brought a welcome spiritual relief to the surviving Jewish inmates. Hardman persuaded the British troops not to bulldoze the cadavers into mass graves but to take time to bury them with "the dignity in death of which they had been robbed in life."

After Belsen, Smith took part in the liberation of Hamburg then pushed on to Berlin, where British forces held back to leave the liberation to Stalin's Soviet forces. On 15 April, 2005, on the 60th anniversary of Belsen's liberation, Smith attended a Holocaust Remembrance service in Hyde Park, where he met a former Belsen inmate, Rudi Oppenheimer, who had been freed from Belsen as a 14-year-old boy.

Glossary

Auschwitz The largest of the Nazi death and slave labor camps, located in southern Poland. At least one million people, mostly Jews, died there.

concentration camps Special prisons operated by the Nazis. The original inmates were political dissidents but, in time, cultural or racial "threats" to Nazi Germany were also imprisoned.

death camps The six special camps in or near occupied Poland where millions of Jews and others were gassed between late 1941 and late 1944. They were also known as extermination camps.

death marches The forced move back to Germany of many surviving Auschwitz prisoners when the Germans abandoned the camp in January 1945. Those who survived the mid-winter marches were generally left at one of Germany's concentration camps.

Einsatzgruppen (special assignment squads) Units of SS men who began the Holocaust by engaging in the mass shooting of Jewish civilians in Soviet Russia in 1941.

General Government of Poland Nazi-occupied Poland, after other portions of the country were annexed by the Soviet Union. The General Government was the geographical center of the Holocaust.

ghettos Mostly in occupied Poland, parts of towns and cities where Jews were quarantined and enslaved until Nazi officials determined what to do with them.

Hoess Action The attempt to murder Hungarian Jews at Auschwitz in the spring and summer of 1944. Named for former Auschwitz commandant Rudolf Hoess (who returned for the occasion), the action required Auschwitz to increase its killing capacity.

The Holocaust

Hiwis Short for "Hilfswillige" or "willing helpers," non-Germans who assisted the Nazis in the Holocaust by standing guard or performing other support tasks. Most were Poles, Lithuanians, or Ukrainians.

Kristallnacht Generally translated as the "Night of Broken Glass," Kristallnacht was a nationwide attack on German Jews carried out mostly by SA and SS members during the nights of November 9-10, 1938. Major targets were Jewish homes, shops, and synagogues, and about one hundred people were killed.

Nuremburg Laws Two anti-Jewish laws announced by the Nazi state in 1935. They removed citizenship rights from Jews, banned sex and marriage between Jews and non-Jews, and defined Jews as any person with three or four Jewish grandparents.

Nuremburg Trial The trial by the four victorious Allied powers (the United States, Great Britain, the Soviet Union, and France) of surviving Nazi leaders in 1945 and 1946. One of the major charges was "crimes against humanity" for measures such as the attempted genocide of European Jews.

Reinhard Action The larger attempt to make Poland "free of Jews," mostly employing the death camps of Belzec, Sobibor, Treblinka, and Majdanek. It was named for SS second-in-command Reinhard Heydrich.

SA (Sturmabteilung) The Nazi Stormtroopers who helped Adolf Hitler come to power and provided mass support thereafter. They were also known as Brownshirts.

SS (Schutzstaffel) Originally Nazi protection squads that evolved into the most powerful organization within the Nazi state under the leadership of Heinrich Himmler who was central to the organization and the carrying out of the Holocaust.

selections A term used by Nazi officials to divide Jewish populations, most frequently into those who would be killed immediately at camps such as Auschwitz or who might, by contrast, be selected for slave labor. Selections were often carried out by Nazi doctors.

Shoah The Hebrew-language word used for the Holocaust.

Sonderkommando Special units of Jewish slaves who worked in and around the gas chambers and crematoria at the death camps.

T-4 program Nazi Germany's euthanasia program in which tens of thousands of Germany's mentally and physically disabled were murdered from 1939 to 1941. It featured the first use of gas chambers.

Theresienstadt A "transit ghetto" located in Nazi-occupied Czechoslovakia and the destination of many Jews with a claim to VIP status, such as German Jews with medals from World War I. Most who were sent there were eventually gassed in one of the death camps in Poland.

Wannsee Conference A meeting held among top SS, Nazi Party, and German state officials in January 1942. Chaired by SS General Reinhard Heydrich, the purpose of the meeting was to announce and begin implementation of the gassing of Jews.

War Refugee Board An organization formed by the US government in January 1944 and designed to try to help Jewish and other refugees from Nazi Germany.

Warsaw Ghetto Uprising The largest example of armed Jewish resistance during World War II, taking place in 1943 in the ghetto of Poland's capital and largest city.

Zyklon B A commercial pesticide made from cyanide gas and modified for use in the gas chambers at Auschwitz.

Organizations to Contact

The editors have compiled the following list of organizations concerned with the issues debated in this book. The descriptions are derived from materials provided by the organizations. All have publications or information available for interested readers. The list was compiled on the date of publication of the present volume; the information provided here may change. Be aware that many organizations take several weeks or longer to respond to inquiries, so allow as much time as possible.

Amnesty International
5 Penn Plaza, 14th Floor
New York, NY 10001
(212) 807-8400 • fax: (212) 463-9193
e-mail: aimember@aisusa.org
website: www.amnestyusa.org

Amnesty International is a worldwide movement of people who campaign for internationally recognized human rights. Its vision is of a world in which every person enjoys all of the human rights enshrined in the Universal Declaration of Human Rights and other international human rights standards. Each year it publishes a report on its work and its concerns throughout the world.

Human Rights Watch
350 Fifth Ave., 34th Floor
New York, NY 10118-3299
(212) 290-4700 • (212) 736-1300
e-mail: hrwnyc@hrw.org
website: www.hrw.org

Founded in 1978, this nongovernmental organization conducts systematic investigations of human rights abuses in countries around the world. It publishes many books and reports on specific countries and issues, as well as annual reports and other articles. Its website includes numerous discussions of human rights and international justice issues.

International Holocaust Remembrance Alliance
Lindenstrasse 20-25 10969
Berlin, Germany
49-30-26396660
e-mail: info@holocaustremembrance.com
website: www.holocaustremembrance.com

The International Holocaust Remembrance Alliance is an intergovernmental body that was established to place political and social leaders' support behind the need for Holocaust education, remembrance, and research—both nationally and internationally.

Shoah Foundation
The Institute for Visual History and Education
650 West 35th Street, Suite 114
Los Angeles, CA 90089-2571
(213) 740-6001
e-mail: vhi-web@usc.edu
website: http://sfi.usc.edu

Affiliated with the University of Southern California, the Shoah Foundation is dedicated to making audio-visual interviews with survivors and witnesses of the Holocaust and other genocides a compelling voice for education and action.

The Simon Wiesenthal Center
1399 South Roxbury Drive
Los Angeles, CA 90035
(310) 553-9036 • (800) 900-9036
e-mail: information@wiesenthal.com
website: www.wiesenthal.com

The Simon Wiesenthal Center is a global Jewish human rights organization that confronts anti-Semitism, hate, and terrorism; promotes human rights and dignity; stands with Israel; defends the safety of Jews worldwide; and teaches the lessons of the Holocaust for future generations. It maintains Museums of Tolerance in both Los Angeles and Jerusalem.

STAND/United to End Genocide
1100 17th Street NW, Suite 500
Washington, DC 20036
(202) 556-2100
e-mail: info@standnow.org
website: www.standnow.org

STAND is the student-led division of United to End Genocide. Its goal is to try to protect ordinary people from persecution and genocide, and it maintains hundreds of chapters at high schools and universities.

United States Holocaust Memorial Museum
100 Raoul Wallenberg Place SW
Washington, DC 20024-2126
(202) 488-0400
website: www.ushmm.org

The United States Holocaust Historical Museum offers general information about the Holocaust, resources for students and researchers, and supports the effort to discourage anti-Semitism and genocide.

Yad Vashem
500 Fifth Ave., 42nd Floor
New York, NY 10110-4299
(212) 220-4304
websites: www.yadvashemusa.org, www.yadvashem.org

Yad Vashem, the Holocaust Martyrs' and Heroes' Remembrance Authority, was established in 1953 by an act of the Israeli Knesset (parliament). Since its inception, Yad Vashem has been entrusted with documenting the history of the Jewish people during the Holocaust, preserving the memory and story of each of the six million victims, and imparting the legacy of the Holocaust through its archives, library, school, museums, and recognition of non-Jews who risked their lives during the Holocaust to save Jews from extermination.

List of Primary Source Documents

The editors have compiled the following list of documents that either broadly address genocide and persecution or more narrowly focus on the topic of this volume. The full text of these documents is available from multiple sources in print and online.

Convention Against Torture and Other Cruel, Inhuman, or Degrading Punishment, United Nations, 1974

A treaty adopted by the United Nations General Assembly in 1974 opposing any nation's use of torture, unusually harsh punishment, and unfair imprisonment.

Convention on the Prevention and Punishment of the Crime of Genocide (UN Genocide Convention), United Nations, December 9, 1948

In the aftermath of the Nazi Holocaust against the European Jews during World War II, the United Nations developed principles defining genocide, as well as measures to prevent it and to punish any perpetrators.

From the Diary of Adam Czerniakow on the Eve of the Deportation from the Warsaw Ghetto, July 20, 1942

The head of the Jewish Council in the Warsaw Ghetto, serving as an intermediary between Nazi officials and the Jewish population, records orders beginning the emptying of the ghetto.

Memorandum Authorizing a "Complete Solution to the Jewish Question," July 31, 1941

Hermann Goering, Nazi Germany's second-in-command, provides SS general Reinhard Heydrich with the authority to solve the Nazi's "Jewish problem" in Eastern Europe.

The Nuremburg Laws, Nazi Party Rally, Nuremburg, Germany, September 15, 1935

Nazi leaders take steps to remove German Jews from public life and to define "Jewishness" based on parentage rather than religion or culture.

The Persecution of the Jews: Methods of Annihilation, 1946

Some of the evidence of the Nazi genocide against Jews presented at the Nuremburg Tribunal.

Principles of International Law Recognized in the Charter of the Nuremburg Tribunal, United Nations International Law Commission, 1950

After World War II (1939–1945), the victorious Allies tried surviving leaders of Nazi Germany in the German city of Nuremburg. The proceedings established standards for international law that were affirmed by the United Nations and by later court tests. Among other standards, national leaders can be held responsible for crimes against humanity, which might include "murder, extermination, deportation, enslavement, and other inhuman acts."

The Program of the National Socialist German Workers' Party, 1920

Leaders of the early Nazi Party, including Adolf Hitler, state their broad aims and blame Jews for some of Germany's problems.

Stroop Report on the Destruction of the Warsaw Ghetto, May 15, 1943

The SS officer in charge of crushing the Warsaw Ghetto Uprising reports on the events to his superiors.

Universal Declaration of Human Rights, United Nations, 1948

Soon after its founding, the United Nations approved this general statement of individual rights it hoped would apply to citizens of all nations.

For Further Research

Books

Robert H. Abzug, *America Views the Holocaust: A Brief Documentary History*. Boston: Bedford/St. Martin's, 2009.

Hannah Arendt, *Eichmann and the Holocaust*. New York: Penguin, 2005.

Mitchell G. Bard, ed., *The Complete History of the Holocaust*. San Diego, CA: Greenhaven, 2001.

Lawrence Baron, *Projecting the Holocaust into the Present: The Changing Focus of Contemporary Holocaust Cinema*. New York: Rowman and Littlefield, 2005.

Christopher R. Browning, *The Origins of the Final Solution: The Evolution of Nazi Jewish Policy, September 1939–March 1942*. Lincoln, NE: Bison, 2007.

David M. Crowe, *The Holocaust: Roots, History, and Aftermath*. Boulder, CO: Westview, 2008.

Lucy Dawidowicz, *The War Against the Jews, 1933–1945*. New York: Bantam, 1976.

Peter Duffy, *The Bielski Brothers: The True Story of Three Men Who Defied the Nazis, Built a Village in the Forest, and Saved 1,200 Jews*. New York: Harper Perennial, 2003.

Deborah Dwork, ed., *Voices and Views: A History of the Holocaust*. New York: The Jewish Foundation for the Righteous, 2002.

Anne Frank, et al., *The Diary of a Young Girl*. London: Bantam Press Reprint, 1997.

Saul Friedlaender, *The Years of Extermination: Nazi Germany and the Jews*. New York: HarperCollins, 2007.

Israel Gutman, *Resistance: The Warsaw Ghetto Uprising.* Boston: Houghton Mifflin, 1994.

Deborah E. Lipstadt, *History on Trial: My Day in Court with David Irving.* New York: HarperCollins, 2005.

Robert G. Moeller, *The Nazi State and German Society: A Brief History with Documents.* Boston: Bedford/St. Martin's, 2010.

Peter Novick, *The Holocaust in American Life.* Boston: Mariner, 2000.

Elie Wiesel, *Night.* Rev. ed. New York: Hill and Wang, 2006.

David Wyman and Rafael Medoff, *A Race Against Death: Peter Bergson, America, and the Holocaust.* New York: The New Press, 2002.

Periodicals and Internet Sources

Ofer Adaret, "For First Time, Rare Warsaw Ghetto Uprising Diaries Unveiled," *Haaretz,* January 17, 2013. www.haaretz.com.

Associated Press, "30 Alleged Auschwitz Guards Could Face Charges," CBC News/Associated Press, September 8, 2013. www.cbc.ca.

"Audio Files of Auschwitz Survivors Go Online," Yahoo News, October 7, 2013. http://news.yahoo.com.

Aaron Berman, "American Response to the Holocaust," History. www.history.com.

Suzanne Daly, "As Germans Push Austerity, Greeks Push Nazi-Era Claims," *New York Times,* October 5, 2013.

Peter Hayes, "Auschwitz, Capital of the Holocaust," *Holocaust and Genocide Studies,* vol. 17, no. 2, 2003.

Srianthi Perera, "As Survivors Slip Away, Call to Teach About Holocaust Grows," *Arizona Republic,* September 16, 2013. www.azcentral.com.

"Remembering the Holocaust: Bearing Witness Ever More," *The Economist,* August 24, 2013.

Henry Rome, "Author Jacobsen Unravels 'Logic' Behind Holocaust Denial, Anti-Semitism," *Jerusalem Post,* October 9, 2013. www.jpost.com.

Timothy Snyder, "A New Approach to the Holocaust," *New York Review of Books,* June 23, 2011.

Lawrence D. Stokes, "From Law Student to Einsatzgruppen Commander: The Career of a Gestapo Officer," *Canadian Journal of History,* April 2002, pp. 1–24.

Matthew Wagner, "An Anchor for National Mourning," *Jerusalem Post,* April 28, 2008.

David Wroe, "Hitler 'Led Henchmen' in Kristallnacht Riots," *Telegraph,* October 21, 2008. www.telegraph.co.uk.

Websites

A Cybrary of the Holocaust (www.remember.org) An online Holocaust library including general historical information, images, audiovisual resources, book summations, and survivors' stories. It also offers discussion forums.

The Holocaust Chronicle (www.holocaustchronicle.org) This website provides a chronological examination of the Holocaust. It features individual stories, photographs, and statistical information.

The Holocaust: Crimes, Heroes and Villains (www.auschwitz.dk) This website, based in Denmark, offers background information on the Holocaust, stories of individuals involved in the event, photographs, timelines, and other materials. It also provides links to other Holocaust-related sites.

Jewish Virtual Library (www.jewishvirtuallibrary.org) A website providing articles, glossaries, maps and other resources on Jewish history. It maintains an extensive section on Holocaust-related subjects.

The Museum of Tolerance (www.museumoftolerance.com) This website is maintained by the Simon Wiesenthal Center and is part of the Museum of Tolerance in Los Angeles. It offers resources for students and teachers and has plans for a virtual museum exhibit.

Films

Auschwitz, the Nazis, and the Final Solution. This is a documentary directed by Laurence Rees and Catherine Tatge, BBC, 2005.

Bearing Witness: The Voices of Our Survivors. This documentary is directed by Heather Elliott Famularo, 2011.

The Counterfeiters. This is a drama directed by Stefan Rusowitzky, Sony Pictures Classics, 2007.

The Grey Zone. This drama is directed by Tim Blake Nelson, Millenium Films, 2001.

Into the Arms of Strangers: Stories of the Kindertransport. This is a documentary directed by Mark Jonathan Harris, Warner Bros., 2001

The Pianist. This drama is directed by Roman Polanski, Focus Features, 2002.

Schindler's List. This drama is directed by Steven Spielberg, Universal Pictures, 1993.

Shoah. This documentary is directed by Franz Lanzmann, New Yorker Films, 1985.

Index

A
Al-Husseini, Mufti Haj Amin, 92
Allendorf concentration camp, 163–164
American Jewish groups, 80
Anielowicz, Mordechai, 81
Anti-Defamation League, 122
Anti-Jewish conspiracy theories, 29
Anti-Semitism
   Aryanization policy, 46–47
   destruction and murder reign, 44–45
   during the Industrial Revolution, 29
   under the Nazi regime, 30
   Nuremburg Laws, 46
   overview, 42–44, *43*
Arbeit Macht Frei (slogan), 73
Arrow-Cross Party, 38
Aryanization policy, 46–47
Assault Detachments (Storm Troopers), 42
Auschwitz concentration camp
   anniversary of liberation from, 108
   arrival at, 72–73, 133–135, 162–163
   Auschwitz trials, 40
   crematoria in, 151
   as death camp, 37, 96, 111
   deportation of Jews to, 37, 160–162
   gas chambers at, 37
   museum, *109*
   as Nazi killing machine, 69
   student visitation to, 72–75
   personal accounts of, 127–135, 149–152
   survivor, *148*
   traveling to, 130–133, 160–161
   US arrival at, 165
Austria
   enforced emigration, 29, 60
   German annexation of, 42, 51
   Jews in, 63
   rioting in, 44
   T4 euthanasia program, 89
Axis Rule in Occupied Europe (Lemkin), 5

B
Baader-Meinhof Gang, 115–116
Babi Yar massacre, 53–55, 102
The Barnes Review (magazine), 114–115
Bartov, Omer, 120, 123
Beer Hall Putsch, 43, 90
Belzec death camp, 34–36, 110
Bengal Famine Mixture, 167
Berenbaum, Michael, 82, 121
Bergen, Doris L., 48–57
Bergen-Belsen concentration camp, 166–168
Berghoff, Hartmut, 68
Biga, Leo Adam, 155–165
Birkenau concentration camp. *See* Auschwitz concentration camp
Bloomfield, Sara, 122
Blumenthal, Nachman, 78
Bolshevism, 50, 56
Bouhler, Philip, 87
Brandt, Karl, 87
British 11th Armoured Division, 167
British National Party (BNP), 114
Bromberg massacre, 102
Bronfman, Edgar, 120

183

Brothels, 69, 71
Browning, Christopher R., 101–107
Buchenwald concentration camp, 45, *70*

C
Cambodia, 8
CANDLES Holocaust Museum and Education Center, 144
Carbon monoxide gas, 35, 97
Carmel, Moshe, 78
Carter, Jimmy, 80–81
Carto, Willis, 114
Catholic Church, 88
Celtic culture, 114–115
Chalk, Frank, 9–10
Chelmno (Kulmhof) camp, 33, 35, 110, *138*
Chvalkovský, František, 90
Clark University, 121
Concentration camps
 brothels in, 69, 71
 ghetto children deported to, 136–139, *138*
 locations of, *74*
 student visitation to, 72–75
 typhus blocks, 153, 167
 See also Forced labor camps
Czechoslovakia, 37, 42, 44, 51, 65

D
Dachau concentration camp, 45, 152–153
Dallaire, Roméo, 11
Daluege, Kurt, 32
Davis, Douglas, 119–123
Davison, Phil, 166–168
Dean, Martin, 70
Death camps
 arrival at, 148–149
 deportations to, 80
 establishment of, 36–37
 euthanasia program, 105
 Jewish children in, 136–139
 medical experiments in, 140
 overview, 110–111
 prussic acid use, 35
 student visitation to, 72–75
 See also Concentration camps; *specific death camps*
Death marches, 39, 152–153
Debrecen ghetto, 163
Denying the Holocaust (Lipstadt), 118
Deportations
 to death camps, 80
 from ghettos, 136–139, *138,* 146
 horror of, 160–162
 Kristallnacht and, 47
 overview, 34–39
 resistance to, 80–81, 128
Diaspora Jews, 77, 82
Dimbleby, Richard, 167
Dinur, Benzion, 77
Dower, John, 102, 104

E
Eichmann, Adolf
 chief administrator of Holocaust, 78
 deportation transports, 38
 "Final solution," 58–66
 interrogation of, 93
Einsatzgruppen (Operation Units)
 Babi Yar massacre, 53–55
 during Final Solution, 96
 introduction, 32
 shootings, 99
 task of, 50, *54*
 trials, 40
Eliach, Yaffa, 52
Emory University, 120
Enforced emigration of Jews
 acceleration of, 59–60, 59–61

Index

policy of, 29, 47, *84*
postwar emigration of survivors, 39
process of, 45, 65
Eyewitnesses to mass murder of Jews, 52–53

F

Far Right Liberty Lobby, 114
Final solution
    decision for, 98–100, *99*
    distribution of Jews, 62*t*
    early statements, 90–91
    evacuation of Jews, 62–66
    Hitler, Adolf, involvement in, 86–93, 98
    overview, 58–62
    post-war recollection over, 93–94
Forced labor camps
    deaths in, 39
    demand for, 36
    number of, 69
    opening of, 111
    selections for, 37–38, 158, 163
    See also Concentration camps; *specific death camps*
Foxman, Abraham, 122
France
    anti-Semitism in, 29
    French Jews, 37, 39, 49
    German-controlled areas in, 68
    ghettos in, 68
    massacre of black soldiers, 49
    registration of Jews, 65
Frank, Anne, 167
Frank, Hans, 35

G

Gas chambers
    builders' specifications for, 109
    death camps, 110
    expansion of, 36–37, 111
    fear of, 149, 160
    Holocaust denial over, 115, 122–123
    prussic acid use, 35
    selection for, 73, 134
    student visitation to, 75
    T4 euthanasia program, 89
    work detail in, 151, 161
Genocide
    defined, 5
    evolving laws of, 8–9
    humanity's recognition of, 5
    legal definition of, 6–8
    motives and early warning signs, 9–11
    prevention and protection, 11–13
Gerlach, Christian, 28–40, 96
German Four-Year Planning Office, 36
German Historical Institute, 68
German Jews, 41–47, 50
Gestapo (Secret State Police), 45, 64, 137–138
Ghettos
    creation of, 65, 159
    deportations from, 136–139, *138*, 146
    documentation of, 67–71
    evacuation of, 160
    gassing in, 110
    home-town ghettos, 69
    overview, 30, 68–69, *99*
    surviving in, 153, 163
    transit-ghettos, 63
    See also specific ghettos
Globocnik, Odilo, 93, 105, 107
Goda, Norman J.W., 76–82
Goebbels, Joseph, 43, 91, 96–98, 100
Göring, Hermann, 36, 45, 97

Graebe, Hermann, 52
Gray, Charles, 120–121
Greenbaum, Henry, 70–71
Griffin, Nick, 114
Gross-Rosen camp, 152
Grynszpan, Herschel, 42
Gur, Mordechai, 77
Gypsy murders, 50–51

H
Habyarimana, Juvenal, 10
Hall of Remembrance (Yad Vashem), 79
Hardman, Leslie, 167
Hasidic Tales of the Holocaust (Eliach), 52
Hebrew Bible, 79
Hell, Josef, 90
Heydrich, Reinhard
  anti-Semitism by, 44
  Einsatzgruppen deployment, 32
  evacuation of Jews, 63–65
  extermination of Jews, 34, 49, 58–59
  Final Solution order, 97
  Reich Security Main Office, 105
Himmler, Heinrich
  death marches, 38–39
  deportation of Jews, 34
  extermination of Jews, 49, 96, 99
  gas use by, 35
  handwritten note by, 92, 98
  head of SS, 64
  influence of, 30
The History and Sociology of Genocide (Chalk, Jonassohn), 9–10
Hitler, Adolf
  authority of, 91–93, *92*
  declaration of war against US, 100
  early statements, 90–91
  extermination of Jews, 34–35, 49
  lost documents, 88–89
  mixed-heritage Jews and, 38
  overview, 5, 10, 86–88
  restore reputation of, 117
  rise to power, 29
  T4 euthanasia program, 87–89
  war against the Jews, 82, 86–94
Hitler Youth, 44
Hoess, Rudolf, 93, 96
Holocaust
  circumstantial causes, 95–100
  consequences of, 39–40
  current thinking on, 96–97
  keeping memory alive, 76–82, 108–112
  lessons learned from, 110–112
  medical experiments, 140–144, *143*
  overview, 28–31, 76–77, 95–96
  recently discovered documents on, 97–98
  shocking nature of, 67–71
  Yad Vashem, 77–79
  See also Deportations; Final solution; Mass murder of Jews
Holocaust deniers
  losing in court, 119–123
  respectable appearance of, 113–118
Holocaust Education Trust, 73
Holocaust Martyrs' and Heroes' Remembrance Authority, 77
Holocaust Martyrs' Forest (Yad Vashem), 79
Holocaust Remembrance Day (*Yom Ha'Shoah*), 77, 81
Holókauton, defined, 28
Horthy, Miklos, 38
Hungarian massacre of Jews, 155–165

Index

Hutu people, 10–11, 111

I
Industrial Revolution, 29
Institute for Historical Review (IHR), 114
International Criminal Court (ICC), 8
Into That Darkness (Sereny), 105
Iraq, 8
Irving, David, 109, 118, 119–120
Israeli Knesset, 77
Israel's Day of Independence, 77
Italian Jews, 37, 128

J
James, Vicky, 74
Japanese attack on Pearl Harbor, 100
Jewish Combat Organization, 80
Jewish Military Union, 80
Jewish Passover holiday, 77, 81
Jewish Police, 137, 146–147
Jewish-Bolshevist system, 56
Jews/Jewish people
   French Jews, 37, 39, 49
   generational trauma, 39–40
   German Jews, 41–47, 50
   Hebrew Bible, 79
   Italian Jews, 37, 128
   mixed-heritage Jews, 38
   overview, 5, 10
   Polish Jews, 30–31, 42
   Slovakian Jews, 37
   Sonderkommando, 151
   Soviet Jews, 31–32, 35
   See also Anti-Semitism; Enforced emigration of Jews; Final solution; Mass murder of Jews
Johannsen, Zoe, 140–144
Jonassohn, Kurt, 9–10

K
Kanzlei des Führers, 35
Kapos, 161–162
Kersten, Felix, 93–94
Khan, Genghis, 9
Killing squads, 49–52
Kindertransport, 50–51
King Edward Camp Hill School for Boys, 74
Kor, Eva Mozes, 140–144
Korczak, Janusz, 79
Kristallnacht
   introduction, 29–30
   Jewish deaths from, 45
   overview, 42–44, *43*
   as turning point, 46–47

L
Lang, Sean, 108–112
Latvia, 32, 51
Lebanon, 8
Lemkin, Raphael, 5
Leuchter, Fred, 115
Levi, Primo, 127–135
Lichtblau, Eric, 67–71
Lipstadt, Deborah, 118, 119–120
Lithuania, 32, 53
Lodz ghetto, 34, 68, *138*, 151
Luther, Martin, 65

M
Mahler, Horst, 115–117
Majdanek death camp, 111, 147–148
Marcus, Barry, 75
Marxism, 29
Mass atrocities/killings, 8, 11–13
Mass murder of Jews
   Babi Yar massacre, 53–55, 102
   eyewitnesses to, 52–53
   German army involvement in, 55–57
   Hungarian massacre, 155–165

The Holocaust

Mass murder of Jews (*continued*)
  killing squads, 49–51
  overview, 49
  Soviet Jews, 31–32
McFee, Gordon, 95–100
Medical experiments on young prisoners, 140–144, *143*
Megargee, Geoffrey, 70–71
Mein Kampf (Hitler), 49
Memorial to Jewish Soldiers (Yad Vashem), 79
Mengele, Josef, 141–144, 161
Michalowsky, Zvi, 52–53
Mixed-heritage Jews, 38
My Lai massacre, 102–103

N
National Democratic Party (NDP), 116
National Socialist Germany, 29, 47, 116–117
Nazi regime
  anti-Semitism under, 30
  control of Europe, *33*
  German passivity, 47
  Gestapo, 45, 64, 137–138
  Hungary relations, 157
  Kristallnacht by, 45
  lost documents of, 88
  unfounded assertions about, 4122
Neo-Nazi skinheads, 115
Netherlands, 37, 39
Noncommissioned officers (NCOs), 104
Nuremburg Laws, 46

O
Oliphant, Will, 72–75
Oppenheimer, Rudi, 167
Order Police, 50–51, 55, 106, 138

P

Pearl Harbor attack, 100
Penguin Books, 121
Pequot people, 10
Pillar of Heroism (Yad Vashem), 79
Poland
  civilian assaults, 49
  death camps in, 105
  German invasion of, 30–31, 33, 35, 65
  German occupation of, 101, 110, 136, 141
  mass killings in, 35, 37, 39
  refugee camps in, 42
  slave labor in, 70
  See also Warsaw Ghetto
Polish Christians, 53
Polish Jews, 30–31, 42
Presidential Commission on the Holocaust, 81
Prisoner-of-war camps, 69, 71
Protestant church, 88
Prussic acid (Zyklon B), 97

Q
Quaker groups, 50

R
Radasky, Solomon, 145–154
Radio Rwanda, 10
Rape crimes, 7–8, 45, 159
Red Army Faction, 115–116
Refugee Children's Movement, 50
Reich Citizenship Law, 46
Reich Security Main Office, 105
Reichenau, Walter von, 56
Reichsgau Wartheland, annex, 33
Reserve Police Battalion
  battlefield frenzy, 102–104
  not dedicated killers, 104–106
  not top Nazis, 106–107
  overview, 102
  pressures of war on, 101–107

Rome Statute of the International Criminal Court, 6–8
Rosh Hashanah (Jewish new year), 53
Rudolph, Germar, 115
Runstedt, Gerd von, 56
Russia
  anti-Semitism in, 29
  camp liberations by, 152, 166
  enforced resettlement, 30
  German invasion of, 100, 151
  ghettos in, 68
  Jewish residents, 61
Russian October revolution (1917), 29
Rutgers University, 120
Rwanda, 8, 111
Ryan, Nick, 113–118

S
Sandberger, Martin, 93
Schmidt, Paul Otto, 92
Secret State Police. *See* Gestapo
Sereny, Gitta, 105
Sex slaves, 71
Shrine of Heroism, 78
Siam-Burma railroad, 103
Sierra Leone, 8
Simon Wiesenthal Center in Israel, 120, 122
Singer, Oscar, 136–139
Six Day War (1967), 79
Slave labor
  battalions, 65
  camps, 36, *70,* 71, 111
  documentation of, 67
  enemy use as, 49
Slovakian Jews, 37
Smith, Adam, 13
Smith, Fred, 166–168
Sobibor death camp, 35–36, 97, 110

Sonderkommando (Jewish slaves), 151
Special Air Service (SAS), 167
SS (Schutzstaffel) paramilitary
  extermination camp plans by, 33–34, 38
  extermination of Jews by, 55, 68, 93, 133
  overview, 45, 47, 49, 64–65
  standards of, 106
  T4 euthanasia program, 35, 89
Stangl, Franz, 105
Star of David, 46, 158
Streckenbach, Bruno, 93–94
Stroop, Juergen, 81
Sweeney, Kevin P., 86–94

T
Taylor, Alex, 74
Tehran Times (newspaper), 120
T4 euthanasia program, 35, 87–89
Tiffany, John, 114–115
Tlomatskie Synagogue, 81
Treblinka death camp, 35, 80, 110, 146, 147
Tutsi people, 10–11, 111
Tutsi Rwanda Patriotic Front, 10
Typhus blocks, 153, 167

U
Uganda, 10
United Nations Convention on the Prevention and Punishment of the Crime of Genocide (UNGC), 5–8
United Nations Security Council, 8
United States Holocaust Memorial Museum, 67, *78,* 79–82, 121, 123

V
Vom Rath, Ernst, 42

W
Waffen-SS Brigades, 32

Wallace, George, 114
Wannsee Conference, 34, 58–66, 97, 98
War Without Mercy: Race and Power in the Pacific War (Dower), 102
Warsaw Ghetto
  home-town ghettos, 69
  overcrowding in, 33
  survival in, 145–147
Warsaw Ghetto Monument (Yad Vashem), 79
Warsaw Ghetto Uprising, 80–81, 147
The Wealth of Nations (Smith), 13
Wilhelm, Hans-Heinrich, 105
World Jewish Congress, 120
World War I, 104, 115
World War II
  death marches, 39
  enforced emigration of Jews, 29
  extermination of Jews, 34, 115
  overview, 5
  war crimes during, 57

Y

Yad Vashem, 69, 77–79
Yahrzeit candles, 130
Yom Kippur War (1972), 79
Yugoslavia, 8, 103, 111
Yugoslavian military internees, 128

Z

Zhukov, Georgi, 100
Zionists, 77, 79, 80, 114, 120
Zundel, Irene and Ernst, 117
Zuroff, Efraim, 120, 123